English FLY HIGH

Boarding

Global Culture Center

English Fly High
Boarding

Copyright © 2015 by Global Culture Center
All rights reserved.

No part of this publication may be reproduced,
stored in a retrieval system, or transmitted in any form or by any means,
electronic, mechanical, photocopying, recording, or otherwise,
without the prior permission of the publisher.

Global Culture Center
www.global21.co.kr
3rd Floor, 577-11, Siheung-daero, Guro-gu, Seoul, Republic of Korea
Tel. 02) 6365 – 5169
Fax. 02) 6365 – 5179

English Fly High - Boarding
Author | Danyeol Moon
Publisher | Sooyeon Lee

Printed in Seoul,
5th Printing - Jul. 2019

ISBN 978-89-8233-253-1 14740
      978-89-8233-250-0 14740 (SET)

About this book

Language learning is like flying an airplane. The first thing that you should do is be equipped with vocabulary and grammar, with which you can assemble the airplane you will eventually fly. The next step is taking off where you will need a huge amounts of energy and practical skills along with courage and a certain degree of concentration and commitment. These primary steps not only need to be carried out with patience on the students' side but also be accompanied with a well-prepared and carefully designed course from the teachers' side. The next step is to fly high with the constant fueling of conversational topics and motivation to the final destination of the proficiency that is required in most standardized spoken tests and interviews of the times. These series of books provide all that is required for the preparation of the flight, guiding the students to acquire the essential volume of vocabulary and expressions and having them internalize the expressions immediately. It also helps students take off into the air, allowing them to actually utilize what they have learned in the previous steps in order for them to get ready for the real-life situations that they will be facing outside of classes. Finally, this series of books will provide them with the essential topics and high-level skills that are crucial in winning a competitive edge in business, as well as in academic pursuits. I hope that everyone who studies with these books will finally be at the destinations that they have been dreaming of.

Danyeol Moon

Contents

Unit	Title	Topic	Function	Grammar
Unit 1 Page 10	How's Everything?	Greetings	- Saying Hello and Goodbye - Asking How People and Things Are	- Be verbs - Contractions
Unit 2 Page 18	Please Call Me Bob.	Introductions	- Talking about Personal Information - Introducing Each Other	- Pronouns (Subject / Object) - Possessive Adjectives
Unit 3 Page 26	I Like Going Camping.	Likes and Dislikes	- Talking about What You Like and Don't Like	- Simple Present - Like[Love, Hate] + Noun / ~ing
Unit 4 Page 34	Is It Snowing?	Weather	- Describing Weather Conditions	- Present Continuous - Possessive Pronouns
Unit 5 Page 42	I'm Going to Visit the Old Palace.	Future Plans	- Describing Future Plans and Intentions - Time Expressions	- Future Tense: Be Going to + Verb

English Fly High | Boarding

Unit	Title	Topic	Function	Grammar
Unit 6 Page 50	Don't Be Nervous.	Appearances Emotions and Feelings	- Describing How People Look - Talking about How You Feel	- Imperatives - Want to + Base verb
Unit 7 Page 58	Where Can I Find the Gas Station?	Directions	- Asking for and Giving Directions Where Some Place Is	- Prepositions of Location - Imperatives
Unit 8 Page 66	I Have a Headache.	Health and Illness	- Explaining Problems with Your Body - Expressing Regrets	- WH-Questions
Unit 9 Page 74	Let's Eat Pizza.	Suggestion	- Suggesting Something and Responding to It - Agreeing with Somebody	- Let's + Base verb - That Sounds + Adjective
Unit 10 Page 82	I Was at Home Yesterday.	Past Actions and Activities	- Asking and Answering Questions about the Past - Describing Physical States and Emotions	- Past Tense of Be verb (Was / Were) - Be Busy ~ing

Answers	Page 90
Appendixes	Page 102

Introduction

1. Words & Expressions

Each unit has a list of words that are essential to the composition of the sentences that demonstrate the key objectives and functions of the unit.

2. Grammar

Grammar is crucial even in a conversation book because it is like the iron beams in a building which sustain and stabilize the whole structure. Through abundant examples and exercises, this book makes sure that Korean adult students are able to comprehend the structure of the sentences that they are supposed to speak before they actually start using them.

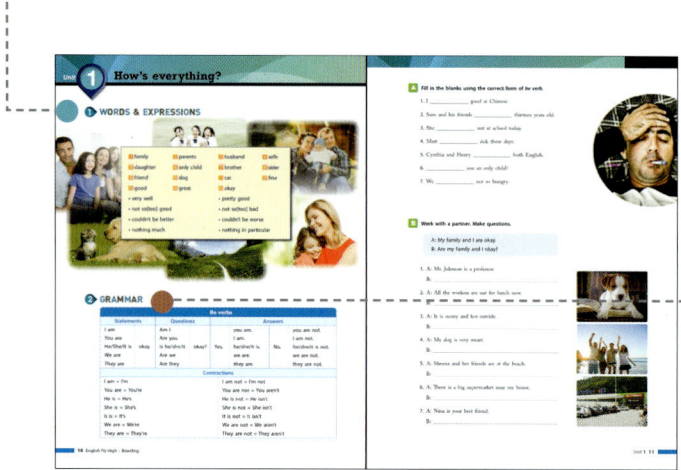

3. Conversation

The conversation exercises have been written based on the principles that the students are fully informed of the context of the interactive language settings and are well-equipped with multiple-intelligence based input as well as opportunities for repetitious practical output performance. Four steps of exercises (A-B-C-D) will help the students gradually and practically build their speaking skills without running out of conversational ideas and expressions. These exercises are easy but they will lead the learners to the objectives of the unit which in most cases means they have fully achieved the comprehension of the grammatical elements and the proficiency in speaking of the target objectives.

4. Reading

Reading must be pleasurable. That means it shouldn't give ESL students a hard time going on and off the text looking up words in the dictionary and wrestling with the meaning of the article. It should be smooth and helping in reinforcing the things that they have newly acquired in the unit. The reading part in this book carries all the features that are portrayed here above. You will enjoy it and you will learn!

Out to the world with Mr. Moon!

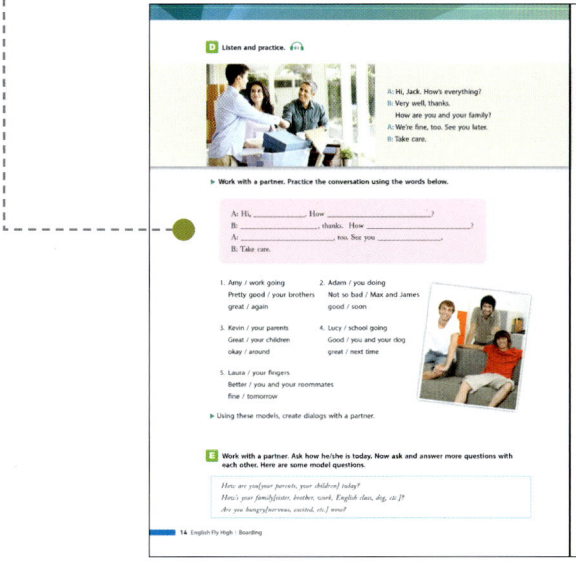

5. Writing

Reception is about mobility whereas production is about fruitfulness. That means that even if you could understand most of the language that is used in this unit, you may not be able to speak or write it on your own, and you could end up not being capable of doing anything "fruitful" for yourself. In most volumes of these books, This "production" part is for speaking.

Unit 1 How's Everything?

LESSON PLAN

 Topic
- Greetings

② **Function**
- Saying Hello and Goodbye
- Asking How People and Things Are

③ **Grammar**
- Be verbs
- Contractions

1. Hi. / Hello.
2. How's everything?
3. Are you a student?
4. How's school going? / How's work going?
5. How are you and your family doing?
6. Are you an only child?
7. How's your brother[sister] doing?
8. How's your dog[cat]?
9. Nice meeting you.
10. See you later. / Goodbye. / Take care.

Unit 1 How's everything?

1 WORDS & EXPRESSIONS

1. family
2. parents
3. husband
4. wife
5. daughter
6. only child
7. brother
8. sister
9. friend
10. dog
11. cat
12. fine
13. good
14. great
15. okay

- very well
- pretty good
- not so[too] good
- not so[too] bad
- couldn't be better
- couldn't be worse
- nothing much
- nothing in particular

2 GRAMMAR

Be verbs							
Statements		Questions		Answers			
I am	okay.	Am I	okay?	Yes,	you are.	No,	you are not.
You are		Are you			I am.		I am not.
He/She/It is		Is he/she/it			he/she/it is.		he/she/it is not.
We are		Are we			we are.		we are not.
They are		Are they			they are.		they are not.
Contractions							
I am = I'm				I am not = I'm not			
You are = You're				You are not = You aren't			
He is = He's				He is not = He isn't			
She is = She's				She is not = She isn't			
It is = It's				It is not = It isn't			
We are = We're				We are not = We aren't			
They are = They're				They are not = They aren't			

A Fill in the blanks using the correct form of *be verb*.

1. I _____ good at Chinese.

2. Sam and his friends _____ thirteen years old.

3. She _____ not at school today.

4. Matt _____ sick these days.

5. Cynthia and Henry _____ both English.

6. _____ you an only child?

7. We _____ not so hungry.

B Work with a partner. Make questions.

> A: My family and I are okay.
> B: Are my family and I okay?

1. A: Mr. Johnson is a professor.
   B: _____

2. A: All the workers are out for lunch now.
   B: _____

3. A: It is sunny and hot outside.
   B: _____

4. A: My dog is very smart.
   B: _____

5. A: Sheena and her friends are at the beach.
   B: _____

6. A: There is a big supermarket near my house.
   B: _____

7. A: Nina is your best friend.
   B: _____

Unit 1 11

3 CONVERSATION

A Work with a partner. Fill in the blanks and practice the conversation below.

A: How **are** you?
B: I**'m** fine, thanks.

A: How _____ you and your family?
B: We _____ fine, thanks.

A: How _____ Dick?
B: He _____ fine, thanks.

A: How _____ your parents?
B: They _____ fine, thanks.

A: How _____ things with you?
B: They _____ fine with me, thanks.

A: How _____ your friend Jane?
B: She _____ fine, thanks.

A: How _____ everything?
B: It _____ fine, thanks.

12 English Fly High | Boarding

B Work with a partner. Fill in the blanks and practice the conversation below.

> A: How are you doing?
> B: I'm doing okay. (okay)

1. A: How _____ Janet doing at work?

    B: _____ (terrible)

2. How _____ Mr. and Mrs. Whitehead doing?

    B: _____ (great)

3. A: How _____ your cat doing?

    B: _____ (very well)

4. A: How _____ you and your husband doing these days?

    B: _____ (okay)

5. A: How _____ your brother doing at school?

    B: _____ (good)

6. A: How _____ your daughter, Maggie, doing?

    B: _____ (pretty good)

C Work with a partner. Practice the conversation using the words below.

school / not too bad

A: How's **school** going?
B: **Not much going on**.

1. work / Nothing much.
2. your diet / Not so well.
3. the new job / Not too bad.
4. the English class / Couldn't be better.
5. your vacation / Couldn't be worse.

Unit 1 13

D Listen and practice.

A: Hi, Jack. How's everything?
B: Very well, thanks.
　　How are you and your family?
A: We're fine, too. See you later.
B: Take care.

▶ Work with a partner. Practice the conversation using the words below.

> A: Hi, _____. How _____?
> B: _____, thanks. How _____?
> A: _____, too. See you _____.
> B: Take care.

1. Amy / work going
   Pretty good / your brothers
   great / again

2. Adam / you doing
   Not so bad / Max and James
   good / soon

3. Kevin / your parents
   Great / your children
   okay / around

4. Lucy / school going
   Good / you and your dog
   great / next time

5. Laura / your fingers
   Better / you and your roommates
   fine / tomorrow

▶ Using these models, create dialogs with a partner.

E Work with a partner. Ask how he/she is today. Now ask and answer more questions with each other. Here are some model questions.

> *How are you[your parents, your children] today?*
> *How's your family[sister, brother, work, English class, dog, etc.]?*
> *Are you hungry[nervous, excited, etc.] now?*

Out to the world with Mr. Moon!

Reading & Writing
Read the conversation below and correct the wrong sentences.

Ben: Hi, Tina. How's it going?
Tina: Pretty good, thanks. And you?
Ben: Very well. By the way, what's that in your hand?
Tina: This is a photo.
Ben: Can I look at it? Who is that beautiful woman?
Tina: She's my sister, Tammy. She's a singer. She's in Las Vegas now.
Ben: A singer?
Tina: Yes. She sings and plays the guitar in clubs.
Ben: Cool.
Tina: She's a great friend and a good listener. I really miss her.
Ben: You have a good sister. Well, nice meeting you, Tina.
Tina: Nice meeting you, too. See you later.

1. Tina has a photo of her brother. ➔ _____
2. Tina has a friend named Tammy. ➔ _____
3. Ben can't look at the photo. ➔ _____
4. Tammy is a dancer. ➔ _____
5. Tammy is in Los Angeles. ➔ _____
6. Tammy plays the piano. ➔ _____
7. Tammy isn't Tina's good friend. ➔ _____

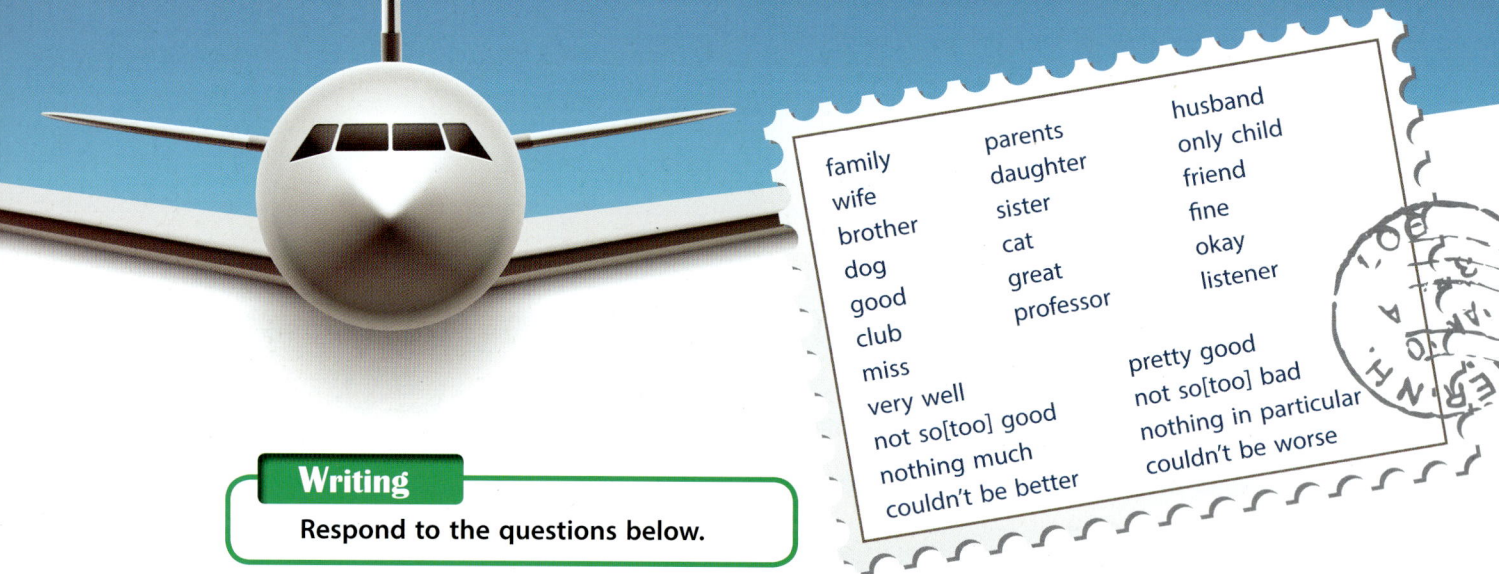

family parents husband
wife daughter only child
brother sister friend
dog cat fine
good great okay
club professor listener
miss
very well pretty good
not so[too] good not so[too] bad
nothing much nothing in particular
couldn't be better couldn't be worse

Writing

Respond to the questions below.

1. Hi. / Hello.

2. How's everything?

3. Are you a student?

4. How's school going? / How's work going?

5. How are you and your family doing?

6. Are you an only child?

7. How's your brother[sister] doing?

8. How's your dog[cat]?

9. Nice meeting you.

10. See you later. / Goodbye. / Take care.

16 English Fly High | Boarding

Unit 2 Please Call Me Bob.

LESSON PLAN

1 Topic
- Introductions

2 Function
- Talking about Personal Information
- Introducing Each Other

3 Grammar
- Pronouns (Subject / Object)
- Possessive Adjectives

1. Can I have your name?
2. What's your first name?
3. What's your family[last] name?
4. How do you spell that?
5. Where are you from?
6. What's your address?
7. Can I have your phone number?
8. What's your e-mail address?

Unit 2 Please call me Bob.

1 WORDS & EXPRESSIONS

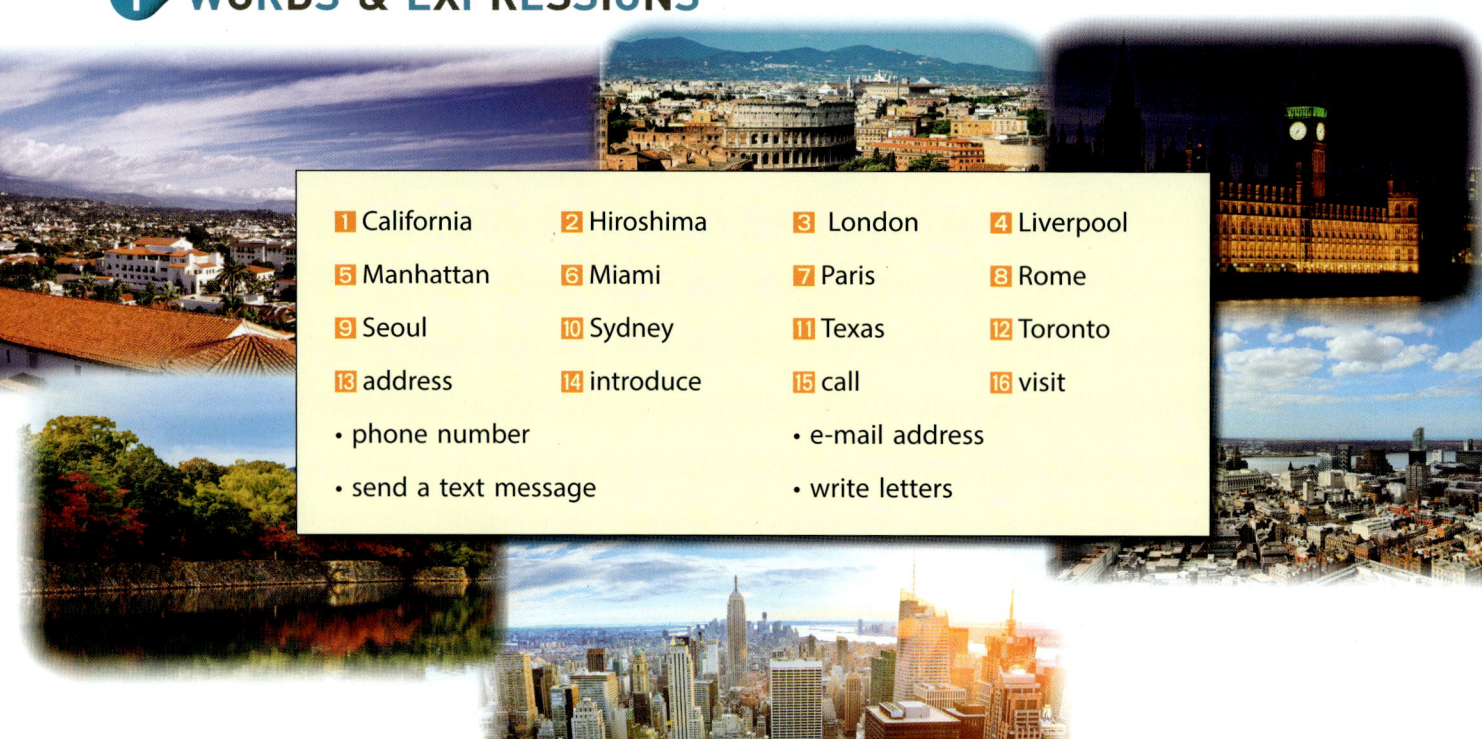

1. California
2. Hiroshima
3. London
4. Liverpool
5. Manhattan
6. Miami
7. Paris
8. Rome
9. Seoul
10. Sydney
11. Texas
12. Toronto
13. address
14. introduce
15. call
16. visit

- phone number
- e-mail address
- send a text message
- write letters

2 GRAMMAR

Pronouns (Subject / Object), Possessive Adjectives			
Subjects	Objects	Possessive Adjectives + Noun	
I	me	my	
you	you	your	
he	him	his	
she	her	her	name
it	it	its	
we	us	our	
they	them	their	

Possessive of Nouns (Noun + 's)	Tom's glasses the boy's brother birds' song

18 English Fly High | Boarding

A Write the correct pronouns or possessive adjectives in the blanks.

> This is Michael's bicycle. It's **his** bicycle.

1. Tom is looking for his friends. Tom can't find _____.

2. I can't see John. I can't see _____.

3. She likes apples. They are _____ favorite fruit.

4. I'm reading the newspaper. I read _____ every day.

5. Mr. Jackson is not here. _____ is out now.

6. Helen is from London. _____ is English.

7. My name is Carolyn Carpenter. Just call _____ Lynn.

B Work with a partner. Replace nouns with pronouns.

> A: **My mom** is making cookies. B: **She** is making cookies.

1. A: **Helen** is from London.
   B: _____

2. A: **My first name** is Kenny.
   B: _____

3. A: Don is talking to **Angela**.
   B: _____

4. A: Where is **Joshua** from?
   B: _____

5. A: **My family and I** are all tall.
   B: _____

6. A: I want to drink **water**.
   B: _____

7. A: **Your dogs** are very friendly.
   B: _____

3 CONVERSATION

A Work with a partner. Fill in the blanks and practice the conversation below.

A: What's your sister's name?
B: <u>Her name is</u> Bridget.

A: What are the boys' names?
B: <u>Their names are</u> Sean and Josh.

A: What's the man's name?

B: _____ Albert.

A: What's your brother's name?

B: _____ Gilbert.

A: What are her dogs' names?

B: _____ Mingky and Funky.

A: What's his girlfriend's name?

B: _____ Dorothy.

A: What are your roommates' names?

B: _____ Anna and Christen.

B Work with a partner. Fill in the blanks and practice the conversation below.

> A: Where are you from?
> B: I'm from Korea.

1. A: _____ Peter from?

   B: _____ from Canada.

2. A: _____ Isabel from?

   B: _____ from France.

3. A: _____ Mr. and Mrs. Cheng from?

   B: _____ from China.

4. A: _____ you and Patrick from?

   B: _____ from Australia.

5. A: _____ Hitomi from?

   B: _____ from Japan.

6. A: _____ Hans from?

   B: _____ from Germany.

C Work with a partner. Practice the conversation using the words below.

David Foster / 755-0818

A: Can I have your name?
B: **David Foster**.
A: How do you spell your last name?
B: F - O - S - T - E - R.
A: Can I have your phone number?
B: It's **755-0818**.

1. Sarah Brightman / 323-2536
2. Josh McQueen / 456-1294
3. Paul Baloche / 987-7643
4. Jane Fonda / 763-0370
5. Peter Strauss / 554-3890
6. Rachel Welch / 879-5542

D Listen and practice. 🎧 03

A: I'm Minho. I'm from Seoul, Korea.
B: My name is Robert Jordan. Please call me Bob.
A: Are you from around here, Bob?
B: Yes, right here in Chicago.

▶ Work with a partner. Practice the conversation using the words below.

> A: I'm _____. I'm from _____.
> B: My name is _____. Please call me _____.
> A: Are you from around here, _____?
> B: Yes, right here in _____.

1. Aaron / Manhattan, America
   Samantha Grant / Sam
   Sam / Liverpool

2. Ben / Sydney, Australia
   Victoria King / Vicky
   Vicky / Toronto

3. Gina / Rome, Italy
   Christopher Reeve / Chris
   Chris / Texas

4. Pierre / Paris, France
   Pamela Anderson / Pam
   Pam / Miami

5. Yukki / Hiroshima, Japan
   Melvin Kate / Mel
   Mel / California

▶ Using these models, create dialogs with a partner.

E Work with a partner. Ask and answer questions with each other. Here are some model questions.

> *What's your name?*   *What's your first name?*
> *What's your family[last] name?* *How do you spell that?*
> *Where are you from?*

Out to the world with Mr. Moon!

Reading & Writing

Read the passage below and answer the questions.

Hello, everyone. I'm your new French teacher. Let me introduce myself. I'm Julie Devoir. I'm thirty years old. I'm from Quebec, Canada. Glad to meet you all. I love French and I want to help you with French. My address is 456 Main Street, Riverside, Philadelphia. My phone number is 010-111-2345 and my e-mail address is French30@school.com. Visit, write, call and text me anytime. You can ask me any questions about French.

1. What's the new French teacher's name?

2. How old is she?
3. Where is she from?
4. What does she want?
5. What's her address?
6. What's her phone number?
7. What's her e-mail address?

Writing

Respond to the questions below.

1. Can I have your name?

2. What's your first name?

3. What's your family[last] name?

4. How do you spell that?

5. Where are you from?

6. What's your address?

7. Can I have your phone number?

8. What's your e-mail address?

Unit 3 I Like Going Camping.

LESSON PLAN

① **Topic**
- Likes and Dislikes

② **Function**
- Talking about What You Like and Don't Like

③ **Grammar**
- Simple Present
- Like[Love, Hate] + Noun / ~ing

1. What do you do in your free time?
2. Do you like sports?
3. What's your favorite sport?
4. Do you like music?
5. What's your favorite music?
6. Do you like animals?
7. What's your favorite animal?
8. Do you like riding a bicycle?

Unit 3 I like going camping.

1 WORDS & EXPRESSIONS

1. badminton
2. baseball
3. basketball
4. boxing
5. tennis
6. soccer
7. guitar
8. history
9. movie
10. piano
11. swim

- classical music
- play cards
- ride a bicycle
- go camping

2 GRAMMAR

Simple Present	
Statements	WH-Questions
I like history.	What subject do you like?
You like history.	What subject do I like?
He/She likes history.	What subject does he/she like?
We like history.	What subject do we like?
They like history.	What subject do they like?
Questions	Answers
Do I like history?	Yes, you do. / No, you don't.
Do you like history?	Yes, I do. / No, I don't.
Does he/she like history?	Yes, he/she does. / No, he/she doesn't.
Do we like history?	Yes, we do. / No, we don't.
Do they like history?	Yes, they do. / No, they don't.

- The verb after he, she, it (3rd person singular) has a final –s.

Like[Love, Hate] + Noun / ~ing
I like[love, hate] books. / I like[love, hate] reading books.

26 English Fly High | Boarding

A Fill in the blanks.

I **like** bananas but I **don't like** apples.

1. You _____ sports but you _____ books.
2. Diana _____ history but she _____ mathematics.
3. Kim _____ his sister but he _____ his brother.
4. We _____ iguanas but we _____ snakes.
5. My sons _____ pizza but they _____ salad.
6. Mike _____ snow but he _____ rain.
7. I _____ birds but I _____ chicken.

B Work with a partner. Write sentences using ~*ing*.

A: I like soccer.
B: **I like playing soccer.**

1. A: Mickey likes badminton.
   B: _____

2. A: My friends like basketball.
   B: _____

3. A: The Jones family like baseball.
   B: _____

4. A: Sam likes the guitar.
   B: _____

5. A: They like the piano.
   B: _____

6. A: Her parents like cards.
   B: _____

7. A: We like the game.
   B: _____

3 CONVERSATION

A Work with a partner. Take turns to ask and answer the questions.

> A: Do you like playing tennis?
> B: Yes, **I like playing tennis**. / No, **I don't like playing tennis.**

A: Do you like cooking spaghetti?

B: No, _____.

A: Does he like swimming?

B: Yes, _____.

A: Does your brother like riding a bicycle?

B: Yes, _____.

A: Does your mother like washing the dishes?

B: No, _____.

A: Do your friends like going camping?

B: Yes, _____.

A: Does Oscar like dancing at the club?

B: No, _____.

B Work with a partner. Take turns to ask and answer the questions.

> A: Do you like coffee?
> B: Yes, I do. I love coffee. /
>   No, I don't. I hate coffee.

> A: Does she like jogging?
> B: Yes, she does. She loves jogging. /
>   No, she doesn't. She hates Jogging.

1. A: _____ you like animals?

   B: Yes, _____. _____

2. A: _____ she like writing letters?

   B: No, _____. _____

3. A: _____ Oliver like cheese?

   B: Yes, _____. _____

4. A: _____ they like going shopping?

   B: No, _____. _____

5. A: _____ you like learning English?

   B: Yes, _____. _____

6. A: _____ Virginia like meat?

   B: No, _____. _____

C Work with a partner. Practice the conversation using the words below.

> **getting up early**
> A: I don't like **getting up early**.
> B: I hate **getting up early**.

1. eating carrots
2. cleaning my room
3. going to the dentist
4. doing my homework
5. moving away
6. making a public speech

Unit 3 29

D Listen and practice.

A: I like math. What's your favorite subject?
B: My favorite subject is music.
A: Why?
B: I like singing and the professor is handsome.

▶ Work with a partner. Practice the conversation using the words below.

> A: I like _____. What's your favorite _____?
> B: My favorite _____ is _____.
> A: Why?
> B: I like _____ and _____ handsome.

1. baseball / sport
   sport / soccer
   watching it / soccer players are

2. classical music / music
   music / rock music
   listening to it / rock singers are

3. history / subject
   subject / English
   speaking English / the teacher is

4. horror movies / movie
   movie / a musical movie
   music / actors are

5. boxing / sport
   sport / bodybuilding
   exercising / bodybuilders are

▶ Using these models, create dialogs with a partner.

E Work with a partner. Ask and answer questions each other. Here are some model questions.

> *Do you like bungee jumping?*　　*Do you like animals?*
> *What's your favorite sport?*　　*Do you like playing basketball?*

Out to the world with Mr. Moon!

Reading & Writing
Read the passage below and correct the wrong sentences.

I'm Billy. I have a dog. His name is Sam. Sam sleeps in the front yard. He gets up early in the morning and stays up very late at night. He loves sausages and bones and he likes barking all day long. He likes chasing birds and cats so he makes a lot of noise. He really likes playing with a ball. I throw a ball and he runs toward it. He loves catching balls. He hates taking a bath so I give him a bath once a week. He really hates it and tries to get out of the bathtub. I love living with Sam.

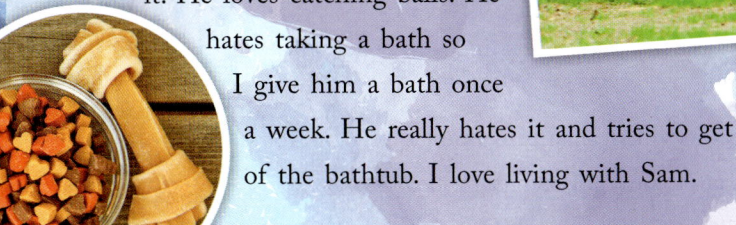

1. The dog's name is Billy. ➡ _____
2. Sam sleeps in the house. ➡ _____
3. He gets up very late. ➡ _____
4. He hates chasing cats. ➡ _____
5. He is very quiet. ➡ _____
6. He really likes playing basketball. ➡ _____
7. He likes taking a bath. ➡ _____

Writing

Respond to the questions below.

1. What do you do in your free time?

2. Do you like sports?

3. What's your favorite sport?

4. Do you like music?

5. What's your favorite music?

6. Do you like animals?

7. What's your favorite animal?

8. Do you like riding a bicycle?

Unit 4 Is It Snowing?

LESSON PLAN

1 Topic
- Weather

2 Function
- Describing Weather Conditions

3 Grammar
- Present Continuous
- Possessive Pronouns

1. How's the weather outside?
2. Is it raining?
3. Do you like sunny days, rainy days, or snowy days?
4. What's your favorite weather?
5. What do you do on snowy days?
6. Do you need a new umbrella or rain boots?
7. What do you like to eat on rainy days?
8. What are you doing now?

Unit 4 Is it snowing?

1 WORDS & EXPRESSIONS

1. sunny
2. fine
3. rainy(raining)
4. pouring
5. storming
6. snowy(snowing)
7. chilly
8. freezing
9. raincoat
10. umbrella
11. rain boots
12. gloves
13. scarf

2 GRAMMAR

Present Continuous / Possessive Pronouns				Possessive Pronouns
Statements		Questions		
I am	eating.	Am I	eating?	mine
You are		Are you		yours
He is		Is he		his
She is		Is she		hers
We are		Are we		ours
They are		Are they		theirs

34 English Fly High | Boarding

A Fill in the blanks.

> Those are Bill's gloves. → They're **his**.

1. This is your car. → It's _____.
2. They're Amy's umbrellas. → They're _____.
3. This is my book. → It's _____.
4. This is our house. → It's _____.
5. These are Paul's glasses. → They're _____.
6. That's Lucy and Jane's room. → It's _____.
7. That is our black and white cat. → It's _____.

B Work with a partner. Write sentences using the *present continuous*.

> A: I eat breakfast at 7 o'clock.
> B: **I'm eating breakfast now.**

1. A: It rains a lot in July.
   B: _____

2. A: She brushes her teeth after breakfast.
   B: _____

3. A: He drinks coffee in the morning.
   B: _____

4. A: We watch TV after dinner.
   B: _____

5. A: I write a diary at night.
   B: _____

6. A: It snows in winter.
   B: _____

7. A: They deliver the newspaper very early.
   B: _____

3 CONVERSATION

A Work with a partner. Take turns to ask and answer the questions.

> A: Is it still raining? (sunny)
> B: No, **it's not raining**. **It's sunny** now.

A: Is it still raining? (cloudy)

B: No, _____. _____ now.

A: Is it still raining? (snowing)

B: No, _____. _____ now.

A: Is it still raining? (windy)

B: No, _____. _____ now.

A: Is it still raining? (fine)

B: No, _____. _____ now.

A: Is it still raining? (freezing)

B: No, _____. _____ now.

A: Is it still raining? (wonderful)

B: No, _____. _____ now.

B Work with a partner. Take turns to ask and answer the questions.

> A: What's the weather like? / How's the weather? (rainy)
> B: It's rainy.

1. A: What's _____? (warm)

   B: _____

2. A: What's _____? (hot)

   B: _____

3. A: What's _____? (cool)

   B: _____

4. A: How's _____? (pouring)

   B: _____

5. A: What's _____? (cold)

   B: _____

6. A: How's _____? (chilly)

   B: _____

C Work with a partner. Practice the conversation using the words below.

it / rain / snow

A: Is it raining?
B: No, it's snowing.

you / watch TV / read a book

A: Are you watching TV?
B: No, I'm reading a book.

1. he / walk / run
2. she / sleep / take a shower
3. they / swim / take a rest
4. you / have a good time / have a terrible time
5. she / cry / laugh
6. he / shout / sing

D Listen and practice. 🎧 07

A: It's raining today.
B: I need a big umbrella. Mine is too small. Can I borrow yours?
A: Of course but mine is not so big.
B: That's okay. Thanks a lot.

▶ Work with a partner. Practice the conversation using the words below.

> A: It's _____ today.
> B: I need _____. Mine _____.
>   Can I borrow yours?
> A: Of course. But mine _____.
> B: That's okay. Thanks a lot.

1. snowing
   big gloves / are too small
   are not so big

2. pouring
   big rain boots / are too small
   are not so big

3. storming
   a big raincoat / is too small
   is not so big

4. freezing
   a big scarf / is too small
   is not so big

▶ Using these models, create dialogs with a partner.

E Work with a partner. Ask and answer questions with each other. Here are some model questions.

> *How's the weather outside?* *Is it raining?*
> *Do you like sunny days, rainy days, or snowy days?* *What's your favorite weather?*
> *What do you do on snowy days?*

Out to the world with Mr. Moon!

Reading & Writing
Read the passage below and answer the questions.

Dear Patty,
Hi, Patty. I'm writing from a hotel in Michigan. The weather isn't good here. It's freezing. I'm looking out the window, and it's snowing a lot. Actually it's a blizzard. I can't go out so I'm just hanging around at the hotel. Right now I'm sitting on the sofa and watching movies on TV. I'm just killing time and doing nothing. I'm so lonely and bored. I'm having a terrible time. What're you doing now, Patty? How's the weather in Florida? Is it sunny? Are you having a good time with your friends? I miss you and I miss the sunny and brisk weather there. I want to see you soon. Bye!
Beth

1. Where is Beth staying in Michigan? ➔ _____
2. Is the weather good in Michigan? ➔ _____
3. What's the weather like there? ➔ _____
4. Can she go out? ➔ _____
5. What is Beth doing right now? ➔ _____
6. Is she having a good time? ➔ _____
7. Where is Patty? ➔ _____

Writing

Respond to the questions below.

1. How's the weather outside?
   _____

2. Is it raining?
   _____

3. Do you like sunny days, rainy days, or snowy days?
   _____

4. What's your favorite weather?
   _____

5. What do you do on snowy days?
   _____

6. Do you need a new umbrella or rain boots?
   _____

7. What do you like to eat on rainy days?
   _____

8. What are you doing now?
   _____

Unit 5 I'm Going to Visit the Old Palace.

LESSON PLAN

1 Topic
- Future Plans

2 Function
- Describing Future Plans and Intentions
- Time Expressions

3 Grammar
- Future Tense: Be Going to + Verb

1. What are you going to do tomorrow?
2. What are you going to do this weekend?
3. What are you going to do on your vacation?
4. What are you going to do on Christmas?
5. What time(When) are you going to get up tomorrow?
6. What time(When) are you going to come home today?
7. What's the weather going to be like tomorrow?
8. Is it going to be sunny tomorrow?

Unit 5 I'm going to visit the old palace.

1 WORDS & EXPRESSIONS

Time

1. 3:00 It's three o'clock.
2. 3:15 It's three-fifteen.
         It's a quarter after three.
3. 3:30 It's three-thirty.
         It's half past three.
4. 3:45 It's three forty-five.
         It's a quarter to four.

5. morning
6. noon
7. afternoon
8. evening
9. midnight
10. today
11. tomorrow
12. Sunday
13. Monday
14. Tuesday
15. Wednesday
16. Thursday
17. Friday
18. Saturday

2 GRAMMAR

Future Tense: Be Going to + Verb			
Subject + Be Going to + Verb		**Questions**	
I am You are He/She is We are They are	going to visit the old palace.	Am I Are you Is he/she Are we Are they	going to visit the old palace?
Answers		**WH-Questions**	
Yes,	you are. I am. he is. she is. we are. they are. No, you aren't. I'm not. he isn't. she isn't. we aren't. they aren't.	What	am I are you is he is she are we are they	going to do?

42 English Fly High | Boarding

A Complete the sentences using *be going to*.

> Jill is thirsty. She **is going to** drink water.

1. I'm hungry. I _____ eat lunch at noon.

2. There are big black clouds in the sky. It _____ rain.

3. She eats too much chocolate. She _____ get fat.

4. Jack has an appointment. He _____ meet his grandfather at 4:30.

5. We're going out. We _____ go to the concert this evening.

6. The bus is leaving. They _____ miss it.

7. I'm going to the party and Brian _____ join me.

B Work with a partner. Write what is going to happen next.

> A: Cindy and Joana are running. (get tired)
> B: **They're going to get tired.**

1. A: My little brother is playing with my cell phone. (break it)
   B: _____

2. A: Paul has no money. (borrow some money)
   B: _____

3. A: It's half past eight. (I / be late for school)
   B: _____

4. A: Morris's sister is sad. (cry)
   B: _____

5. A: I'm buying a present. (give it to my friend)
   B: _____

6. A: We want to wash our hands. (go to the bathroom)
   B: _____

7. A: You are studying very hard. (pass the examination)
   B: _____

Unit 5 43

3 CONVERSATION

A Work with a partner. Practice the conversation using the sentences below.

> A: What time(When) **is** Cathy going to get up tomorrow morning?
> B: **She's going to get up** at 6 o'clock.

1. A: What time _____ you going to come home today?
   B: _____ at 7:00.

2. A: When _____ they going to get together tonight?
   B: _____ at 10:30.

3. A: What time _____ we going to eat dinner this evening?
   B: _____ at 7:30.

4. A: When _____ the train going to leave this afternoon?
   B: _____ at 1:15.

5. A: What time _____ the plane going to arrive this evening?
   B: _____ at 8:00.

6. A: When _____ they going to have the party today?
   B: _____ at noon.

44 English Fly High | Boarding

B Work with a partner. Take turns to ask and answer the questions.

> A: Is it going to be sunny tomorrow?
> B: No, it isn't. It's going to be rainy.

1. **hot / cool**

   A: Is it going to be _____ tomorrow?

   B: No, it isn't. _____

2. **sunny / snowy**

   A: Is it going to be _____ tomorrow?

   B: No, it isn't. _____

3. **cloudy / sunny**

   A: Is it going to be _____ tomorrow?

   B: No, it isn't. _____

4. **warm / cold**

   A: Is it going to be _____ tomorrow?

   B: No, it isn't. _____

5. **chilly / warm**

   A: Is it going to be _____ tomorrow?

   B: No, it isn't. _____

6. **rainy / fine**

   A: Is it going to be _____ tomorrow?

   B: No, it isn't. _____

C Work with a partner. Practice the conversation using the words below.

> A: What are you going to do this weekend?
> B: I'm going to go to the beach.

1. Dick / visit the old palace
2. you and your family / go camping
3. Emma and Daniel / go to the concert
4. Annette / do some grocery shopping
5. you / move out
6. your parents / clean the garage

D Listen and practice.

A: Hi, Jack! Where are you going?
B: I'm going to the airport. I'm going to pick up my mother at 5:30 there. What time is it?
A: It's 5 o'clock already.
B: Oops! I'm sorry, but I have to leave now. See you later.

▶ Work with a partner. Practice the conversation using the words below.

> A: Hi, _____! Where are you going?
> B: I'm going to _____. I'm going to _____.
>   What time is it?
> A: It's _____ already.
> B: Oops! I'm sorry, but I have to leave now. See you later.

1. Betty
   the park
   take a walk before 7 o'clock
   6:30 (six-thirty / half after six)

2. Warren
   the post office
   send the parcel by 5 o'clock
   4:45 (four forty-five/ a quarter to five)

3. Kevin
   the restaurant
   have lunch with somebody at 1 o'clock
   12:55 (twelve fifty-five / five to one)

4. Max
   the supermarket
   buy some bananas before 4 o'clock
   3:40 (three-forty)

▶ Using these models, create dialogs with a partner.

E Work with a partner. Look at the planner below. Take turns to ask and answer about what you're going to do.

Weekly Planner

Sunday	1st April	Go to church
Monday	2nd April	Exercise at the gym
Tuesday	3rd April	Eat out with Grace
Wednesday	4th April	Go to the dentist
Thursday	5th April	Buy a birthday present for Colin
Friday	6th April	Do the grocery shopping
Saturday	7th April	Clean the house

A: What are you going to do on Monday (April 2nd)?   B: I'm going to exercise at the gym.

Out to the world with Mr. Moon!

Reading & Writing

Read the conversation below and answer the questions.

Max: You look lost. Can I help you?
Cindy: Yes. This is my first day on campus. Where is the student cafeteria?
Max: I'll take you there. I'm Max Carpenter.
Cindy: My name's Cindy, Cindy Last. Where are you from, Max?
Max: I'm from right here in Boston. Are you from around here, too?
Cindy: No. I'm from Kansas.
Max: So how do you like Boston and the university?
Cindy: You know. Everything is different.
Max: Well, you're going to get used to it. Oh, here you are. I'm going to eat lunch. Aren't you going to join me?
Cindy: Yes, I am. Thanks.

1. What is Cindy looking for? ➔ _____
2. What is Max going to do for Cindy? ➔ _____
3. What is Cindy's family name? ➔ _____
4. Where is Max from? ➔ _____
5. Where is Cindy from? ➔ _____
6. What is Max going to do at the student cafeteria?
   ➔ _____
7. Is Cindy going to join Max? ➔ _____

Unit 5 47

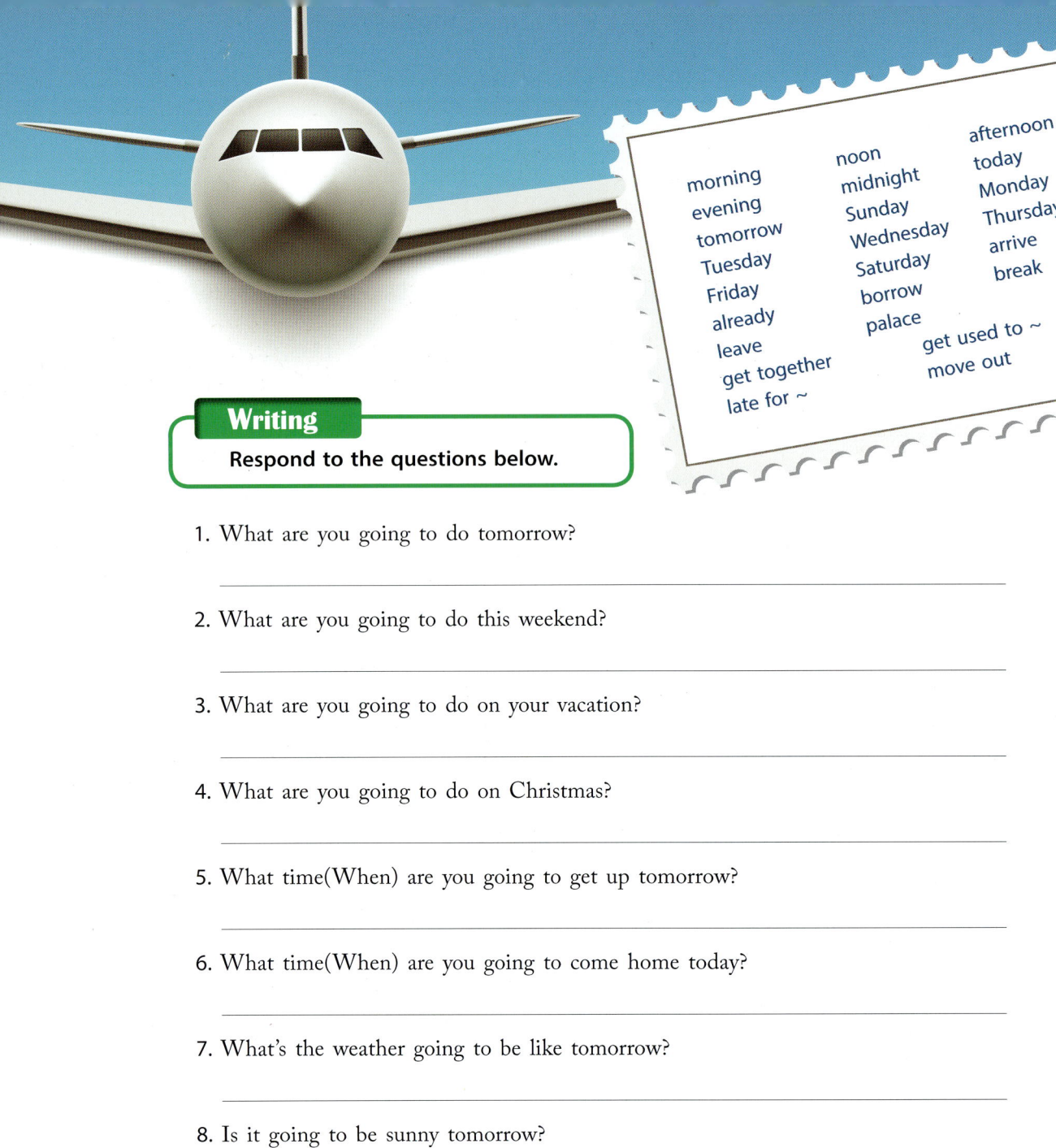

Writing

Respond to the questions below.

1. What are you going to do tomorrow?

2. What are you going to do this weekend?

3. What are you going to do on your vacation?

4. What are you going to do on Christmas?

5. What time(When) are you going to get up tomorrow?

6. What time(When) are you going to come home today?

7. What's the weather going to be like tomorrow?

8. Is it going to be sunny tomorrow?

Unit 6 Don't Be Nervous.

LESSON PLAN

1 Topic
- Appearances
- Emotions and Feelings

2 Function
- Describing How People Look
- Talking about How You Feel

3 Grammar
- Imperatives
- Want to + Base verb

1. How does your English teacher look today?
2. Is he/she tall?
3. Does he/she have long hair or short hair?
4. Is his/her hair straight or curly?
5. What color is his/her hair?
6. What color are his/her eyes?
7. What is he/she wearing today?
8. Is he/she wearing glasses?

Unit 6 Don't be nervous.

1 WORDS & EXPRESSIONS

1. cute
2. charming
3. handsome
4. gorgeous
5. shy
6. sad
7. angry
8. nervous
9. embarrassed
10. scared
11. cry
12. panic
13. relax

- tall - short
- chubby - thin[slim, slender]
- straight hair - curly hair

2 GRAMMAR

	Imperatives: (Subject) Verb + Modifier	
	Positives	Negatives
(You)	Come here.	Don't come here.
	Be quiet.	Don't be quiet.

Want to + Base verb					
Positives		Negatives		Questions	
I You We They	want to study abroad.	I You We They	don't want to study abroad.	Do	I you we they	want to study abroad?
He She	wants to study abroad.	He She	doesn't want to study abroad.	Does	he she	want to study abroad?

Colors								
white	yellow	orange	pink	red	green	blue	purple	gray	black

A Fill in the blanks using *want, wants, do, does, to*.

1. I _____ this pink bag.

2. Abby _____ to buy the black shoes.

3. We want _____ go to bed early.

4. _____ Dennis want to play basketball?

5. Eva _____ to have blue eyes.

6. _____ you want to wear the blue jeans?

7. My children want _____ eat out this evening.

B Work with a partner. Turn the positive imperatives into negatives and the negatives into positives.

| Listen. | ➡ | Don't listen. |
| Don't open the door. | ➡ | Open the door. |

1. Sit down. ➡ _____

2. Don't go to sleep. ➡ _____

3. Say hello to her. ➡ _____

4. Don't shut the window. ➡ _____

5. Watch TV all day long. ➡ _____

6. Don't always smile. ➡ _____

7. Get up late. ➡ _____

3 CONVERSATION

A Work with a partner. Fill in the blanks and practice the conversation below.

A: I'm sad because I'm sick. (get some rest)
B: <u>Don't be sad</u>. <u>Just get some rest</u>.

A: I panic because I'm scared. (relax)
B: <u>Don't panic</u>. <u>Just relax</u>.

A: I'm angry because I'm hungry. (eat something)
B: _____. _____

A: I'm embarrassed because there're so many people. (take it easy)
B: _____. _____

A: I'm nervous because I have an interview. (make yourself at home)
B: _____. _____

A: I blush because Albert is over there. (say hello to him)
B: _____. _____

A: I cry because I'm sad. (cheer up)
B: _____. _____

B Work with a partner. Fill in the blanks and practice the conversation.

> **Julie / blond hair**
> A: Is Julie the one with blond hair?
> B: Yes, she has blond hair.

> **your brothers / brown hair**
> A: Are your brothers the ones with brown hair?
> B: Yes, they have brown hair.

1. **John / black hair**
   A: _____
   B: Yes, _____.

2. **Bridget / blue eyes**
   A: _____
   B: Yes, _____.

3. **Tom's sisters / curly hair**
   A: _____
   B: Yes, _____.

4. **Karen / straight hair**
   A: _____
   B: Yes, _____.

5. **his children / red hair**
   A: _____
   B: Yes, _____.

6. **Brad / brown eyes**
   A: _____
   B: Yes, _____.

C Work with a partner. Practice the conversation using the words below.

> A: How does Shirley look?
> B: She looks charming.

> A: How do they look?
> B: They look awesome.

1. I / great
2. Andy / cute
3. his sisters / wonderful
4. Abigail / gorgeous
5. Clark / handsome
6. Daisy / beautiful

Unit 6 53

D Listen and practice. 🎧 11

A: Do you see the tall girl with blue jeans? I like her.
B: The one with blond hair? She looks gorgeous. Say hello to her.
A: I want to but I can't. I'm so nervous.
B: Don't be nervous. Be brave!

▶ Work with a partner. Practice the conversation using the words below.

A: Do you see the _____ girl with _____? I like her.
B: The one with _____ hair? She looks _____.
   Say hello to her.
A: I want to but I can't. _____
B: Don't _____. Be brave!

1. short / blue skirt
   black / cute
   I'm so shy.
   be shy

2. thin / white skirt
   curly / pretty
   I'm so embarrassed.
   be embarrassed

3. slender / pink blouse
   straight / nice
   I'm so scared.
   be scared

4. chubby / brown sweater
   long / wonderful
   I blush.
   blush

5. slim / orange shorts
   short / great
   I panic.
   panic

▶ Using these models, create dialogs with a partner.

E Work with a partner. Take turns to tell each other what to do, and do it. See the list below for some ideas.

stand up	sit down	laugh	cry	put your hands on your head
open your mouth	close your mouth	open your eyes		close your eyes
close one eye	count to ten	stand on one leg		bark like a dog

Partner A: Stand up. (Partner B stands up.)
Partner B: Put your hands on your head. (Partner A puts his/her hands on his/her head.)

Out to the world with Mr. Moon!

Reading & Writing
Read the passage below and correct the wrong sentences.

Sally wants to be slim just like all the other women and she wants to look gorgeous. She's trying very hard for her health. She always follows rules like these. Don't' skip breakfast. Don't eat fast food too often. Eat a lot of vegetables and fruit. Don't drive. Walk a lot. Don't take elevators. Take stairs. She doesn't want to eat junk food. She likes drinking green tea, because she wants to lose weight and relax.

1. Sally doesn't want to be slim and look gorgeous.
   → _____
2. She isn't trying hard for her health. → _____
3. She always skips breakfast. → _____
4. She really likes fast food. → _____
5. She takes elevators instead of stairs. → _____
6. She wants to eat junk food. → _____
7. She likes drinking coffee. → _____

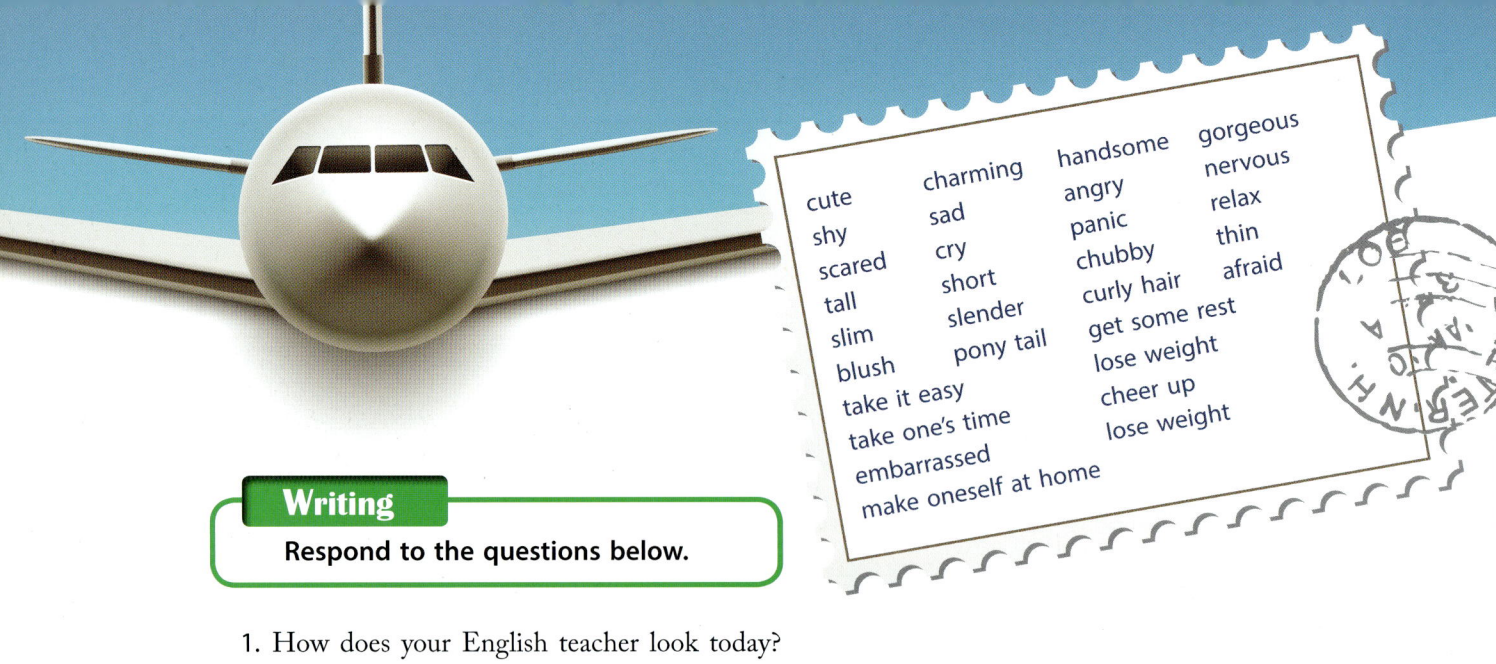

Writing

Respond to the questions below.

1. How does your English teacher look today?
   _____

2. Is he/she tall?
   _____

3. Does he/she have long hair or short hair?
   _____

4. Is his/her hair straight or curly?
   _____

5. What color is his/her hair?
   _____

6. What color are his/her eyes?
   _____

7. What is he/she wearing today?
   _____

8. Is he/she wearing glasses?
   _____

Unit 7 — Where Can I Find the Gas Station?

LESSON PLAN

1. **Topic**
   - Directions

2. **Function**
   - Asking for and Giving Directions Where Some Place Is

3. **Grammar**
   - Prepositions of Location
   - Imperatives

1. Where is your house?
2. What is there next to your house?
3. What is there across from your house?
4. Is there a bank in your neighborhood?
5. What's the name of the bank near your house?
6. Where are you now?
7. Is there a subway station around here?
8. Can you tell me the way to the subway station from here?

Unit 7 Where can I find the gas station?

1 WORDS & EXPRESSIONS

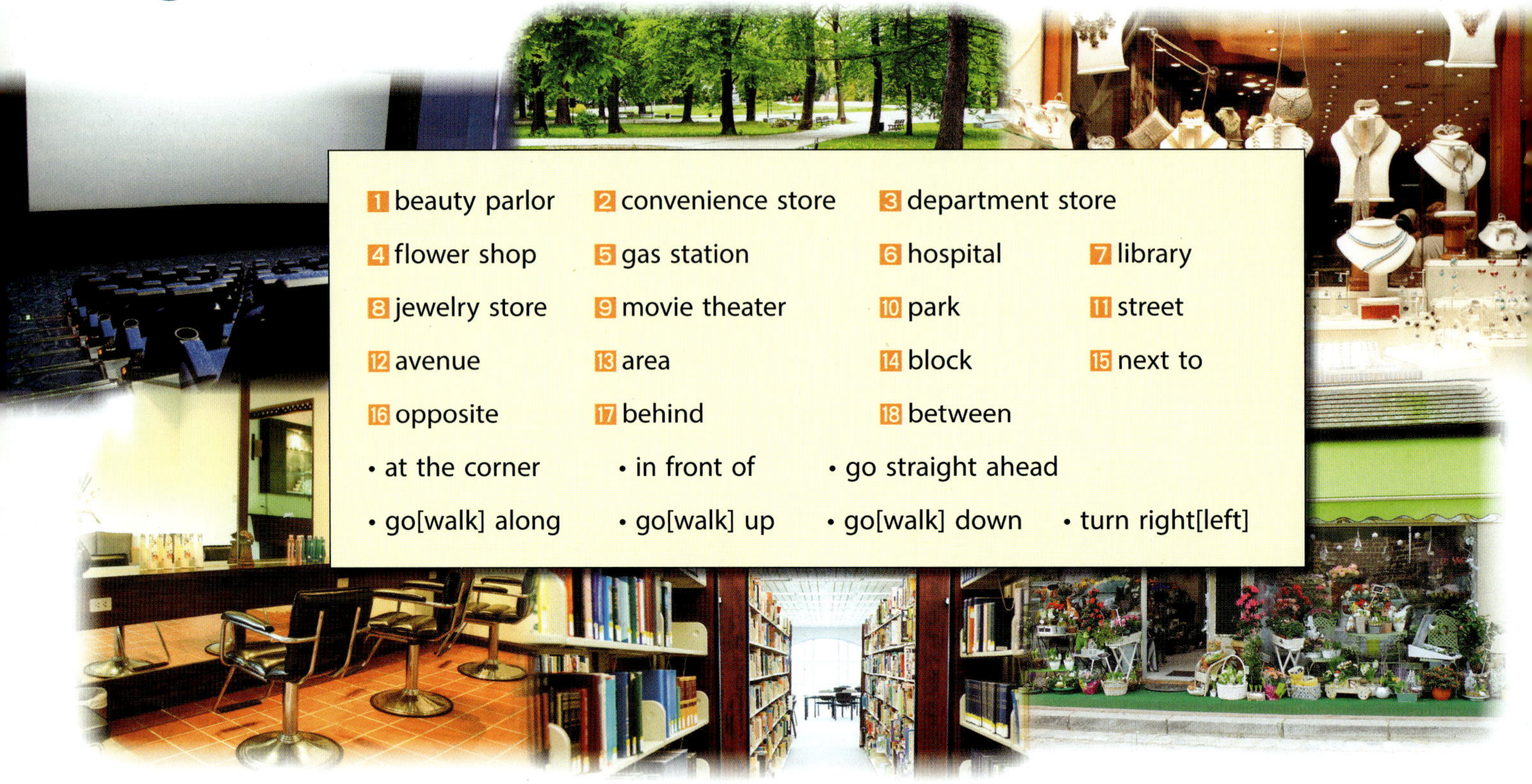

- 1 beauty parlor
- 2 convenience store
- 3 department store
- 4 flower shop
- 5 gas station
- 6 hospital
- 7 library
- 8 jewelry store
- 9 movie theater
- 10 park
- 11 street
- 12 avenue
- 13 area
- 14 block
- 15 next to
- 16 opposite
- 17 behind
- 18 between

- at the corner
- in front of
- go straight ahead
- go[walk] along
- go[walk] up
- go[walk] down
- turn right[left]

2 GRAMMAR

Prepositions of Location	
on + (name of the street)	at + (address number)
The library is on Main Street.	My office is at 123 Maple Street.
next to, across from(opposite), in front of, behind, between ~ and ~	
The bank is next to[across from, in front of, behind] the library. The bank is between the library and the bakery.	
Imperatives: (Subject) Verb + Modifier	
(You) Turn right. / (You) Turn left. Go along[up, down, straight ahead].	

Asking for Directions	
Where is the gas station? Where can I find the gas station? How can I get to the gas station?	Go up First Avenue to Main Street. Turn right and go straight ahead to Second Avenue. The gas station is on the right.
Can you tell me the way to the gas station? Can you show me the way to the gas station?	
Is there a gas station around here?	

A Make questions.

> **There is** a park around here. → **Is there** a park around here?

1. There is a flower shop around here. → _____
2. There are jewelry stores near here. → _____
3. There is a library on First Avenue. → _____
4. There are convenience stores in this area. → _____
5. There is a shopping mall on Maple Street. → _____
6. There are pay phones in this neighborhood. → _____
7. There is a subway station on the corner. → _____

B Work with a partner. Take turns to change sentences like below.

> A: Where is the library? → B: Where can I find the library?

1. A: Where is the bank?
   B: _____

2. A: Where is the post office?
   B: _____

3. A: Where are the book stores?
   B: _____

4. A: Where is the bus stop?
   B: _____

5. A: Where are the convenience stores?
   B: _____

6. A: Where is the hospital?
   B: _____

7. A: Where is the department store?
   B: _____

3 CONVERSATION

A Work with a partner. Fill in the blanks and practice the conversation below.

> A: Where **is** your house?
> B: **It's at** 3395 Central Street. / **It's on** Central Street.

A: Where _____ your office?

B: _____ Main Street.

A: Where _____ the gas station?

B: _____ 256 First Avenue.

A: Where _____ the beauty parlor?

B: _____ Central Street.

A: Where _____ the pay phones?

B: _____ Second Avenue.

A: Where _____ the library?

B: _____ 7935 Maple Street.

A: Where _____ the drug store?

B: _____ Third Avenue.

B Work with a partner. Take turns to ask and answer the questions.

> A: I'm new here. Is there a gas station around here?
> B: Yes, there is. Go straight ahead.

1. convenience store / Go straight two blocks.

2. department store / Turn right at the corner.

3. subway station / Turn left at the corner.

4. hospital / Go along Main Street.

5. movie theater / Go down Central Avenue.

6. jewelry store / Go up First Street.

C Work with a partner. Practice the conversation using the words below.

> A: Excuse me. **Can you tell me the way** to the park?
> B: Sure. **Go down** Central Street to First Avenue and **turn right**.

1. Can you tell me the way / Go up / turn left
    A: Excuse me. _____ to the park?
    B: Certainly. _____ Central Street to
       First Avenue and _____.

2. Can you show me the way / Go along / turn right
    A: Excuse me. _____ to the park?
    B: Of course. _____ Central Street to
       First Avenue and _____.

3. Please tell me how to get / Walk up / turn left
    A: Excuse me. _____ to the park?
    B: Certainly. _____ Central Street to
       First Avenue and _____.

4. Please show me the way / Walk down / turn right
    A: Excuse me. _____ to the park?
    B: Of course. _____ Central Street to
       First Avenue and _____.

Unit 7 61

D Listen and practice.

A: Where can I find the hospital?
B: Do you see that building?
A: Do you mean the old grey one?
B: That's the library and the hospital is right next to it. You can't miss it.

▶ Work with a partner. Practice the conversation using the words below.

> A: _____
> B: Do you see that building?
> A: Do you mean the _____ one?
> B: That's the library. And the hospital is _____.
>   You can't miss it.

1. How can I get to the hospital?
   white new
   in front of it

2. Where is the hospital?
   old wooden
   behind it

3. Can you tell me the way to the hospital?
   new concrete
   across from it

4. Can you show me the way to the hospital?
   old small
   opposite to it

▶ Using these models, create dialogs with a partner.

E Work with a partner. Ask for and give directions like the model dialog.

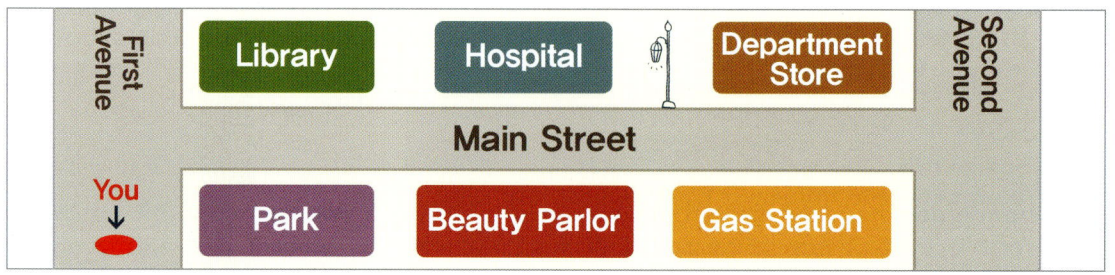

A: How can I get to the library?
B: Go up First Avenue to Main Street and turn right at the corner. It's on your left.

62 English Fly High | Boarding

Out to the world with Mr. Moon!

Reading & Writing
Read the dialog below and correct the wrong sentences. 🎧 14

Donald: I'm new here. Can you tell me how to get to the movie theater?

Joseph: Sorry. I'm a stranger here myself. My friend, Lucy, can help you. She lives here. Where is the movie theater, Lucy?

Lucy: It's on Main Street next to the library.

Donald: Where is the library?

Lucy: It's across from the hospital.

Donald: Don't be angry but how can I get to the hospital?

Lucy: Go up Second Avenue to Main Street and turn left. You can see the big white building. It's the hospital and the movie theater is opposite to it.

Donald: Thank you very much.

Lucy: You're welcome. You can't miss it. Have a good time!

1. Joseph is looking for the movie theater. ➡ _____
2. Joseph knows where the movie theater is. ➡ _____
3. Lucy is Donald's friend. ➡ _____
4. The movie theater is on Central Avenue next to the library.
   ➡ _____
5. The library is next to the hospital. ➡ _____
6. Lucy is angry at Donald. ➡ _____
7. The big white building on Main Street is the movie theater.
   ➡ _____

Unit 7 63

beauty parlor
department store
gas station
jewelry store
park
area
next to
behind
go[walk] along
go[walk] up
turn right[left]
convenience store
flower shop
movie theater
library
street
block
opposite
between
go straight ahead
go[walk] down
at the corner
hospital
avenue
in front of

Writing

Respond to the questions below.

1. Where is your house?

2. What is there next to your house?

3. What is there across from your house?

4. Is there a bank in your neighborhood?

5. What's the name of the bank near your house?

6. Where are you now?

7. Is there a subway station around here?

8. Can you tell me the way to the subway station from here?

Unit 8 — I Have a Headache.

LESSON PLAN

1 Topic
- Health and Illness

2 Function
- Explaining Problems with Your Body
- Expressing Regrets

3 Grammar
- WH-Questions

1. How do you feel today?
2. How are you feeling now?
3. What's the matter? / What's wrong?
4. Do you have a cold?
5. Is your throat sore?
6. When are you going to get a medical checkup?
7. Who's your doctor?
8. How do you get to your doctor's office?

Unit 8 I have a headache.

1 WORDS & EXPRESSIONS

1. cold
2. fever
3. sore throat
4. cough
5. runny nose
6. stuffy nose
7. headache
8. backache
9. stomachache
10. toothache
11. earache

2 GRAMMAR

WH-Questions: What, Who, Where, When, Why, How			
Questions	Verbs	Subjects	Verbs
What	is	your name?	
Who	are	you?	
Where	are	you?	
When	is	your birthday?	
What	do	you	do?
Where	does	he	live?
When	does	she	go to bed?
Why	do	they	study?
How	do	you	feel?

Questions	Verbs	Subjects	Verbs
What	are	you	doing?
Who	is	he	watching?
Where	are	you	going?
When	is	she	going to marry?
Why	are	you	crying?
How	are	you	feeling?

Sickness

I/You/We/They have a cold[fever, cough, headache, toothache, etc.].
He/She has a cold[fever, cough, headache, toothache, etc.].

A Write the correct question word.

> **How** do you go to school?

1. _____ is the hospital? Is it next to the library?
2. _____ is wrong with you? You look awful.
3. _____ do you feel today?
4. _____ is George absent today?
5. _____ does the doctor's office open? Does it open at 9:30 or 10 o'clock?
6. _____ is your family doctor? Is it Dr. Jones?
7. _____ are you coughing?

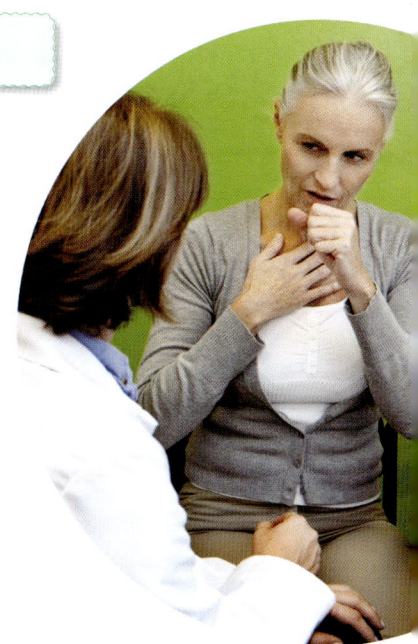

B Work with a partner. Answer the questions by completing the sentences.

A: How is he feeling today?
B: **He's** feeling well.

1. A: Where is the hospital?
   B: _____ across from the bank.

2. A: When are you going to see a doctor?
   B: _____ going to see him tomorrow.

3. A: How do you get to the clinic?
   B: _____ to the clinic by subway.

4. A: What does Dorothy do?
   B: _____ a doctor.

5. A: Who are you?
   B: _____ your father.

6. A: How does your uncle feel?
   B: _____ terrible.

7. A: Why are they laughing?
   B: Because _____ happy.

3 CONVERSATION

A Work with a partner. Fill in the blanks and practice the conversation below.

A: How does Abel feel?
B: **He feels** fine.

A: How are you feeling?
B: **I'm feeling** good.

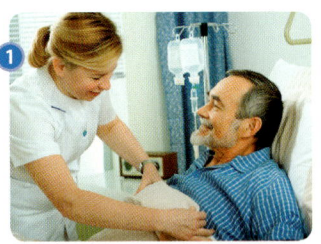

A: How do you feel?

B: _____ great.

A: How does your grandmother feel?

B: _____ bad.

A: How is Brian feeling?

B: _____ well.

A: How do your parents feel?

B: _____ okay.

A: How are Mr. and Mrs. Clark feeling?

B: _____ terrible.

A: How is Gary feeling?

B: _____ wonderful.

68 English Fly High | Boarding

B Work with a partner. Take turns to ask and answer the questions.

> **cold**
> A: What's the matter with you?
> B: I have a cold.

1. **fever**
   A: What's the matter with Lindsey?
   B: _____

2. **headache**
   A: What's the matter with Maria?
   B: _____

3. **runny nose**
   A: What's the matter with your brother?
   B: _____

4. **earache**
   A: What's the matter with you?
   B: _____

5. **stuffy nose**
   A: What's the matter with Charlie?
   B: _____

6. **cough**
   A: What's the matter with you and your husband?
   B: _____

C Work with a partner. Practice the conversation using the words below.

A: How do you feel today?
B: <u>I feel great</u>.
A: I'm glad to hear that.

A: How do you feel today?
B: <u>I feel terrible</u>.
A: I'm sorry to hear that.

1. I feel fine.
2. I feel awful.
3. I feel okay.
4. Not so good.
5. I feel good.
6. Not so well.

D Listen and practice.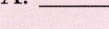

A: How do you feel?
B: Not so good.
A: What's wrong?
B: I have a bad cold.
A: That's too bad.

▶ Work with a partner. Practice the conversation using the words below.

A: How do you feel?
B: _____
A: What's _____?
B: I have a _____.
A: _____

1. Not so well.
   the matter
   headache
   I'm sorry to hear that.

2. I don't feel good.
   wrong
   backache
   That's too bad.

3. Not so great.
   the matter
   fever
   I'm sorry to hear that.

4. I don't feel well.
   wrong
   toothache
   That's too bad.

5. Not so good.
   the matter
   sore throat
   I'm sorry to hear that.

▶ Using these models, create dialogs with a partner.

E Work with a partner. Suppose you're at the doctor's office. You're a doctor and your partner is a patient. Take turns to ask and answer the questions. Here is a model dialog.

A: How do you feel today?
B: I feel terrible.
A: What's the matter?
B: I have a cold.
A: Do you have any other problems?
B: I have a fever and sore throat.

Out to the world with Mr. Moon!

Reading & Writing
Read the passage below and answer the questions.

Donna isn't feeling well today. She has a fever and headache. Her throat is really sore and her nose is runny. She even has an earache. She can do nothing at all. She has to take a day off today. She is going to see the doctor this afternoon. Her family doctor is Mr. Brown but he's on vacation today so she's going to see Dr. Bell. She can't drive her car by herself today because she's very sick. She's going to the doctor's office by taxi. She's a little nervous. She doesn't want to have the terrible flu.

1. How is Donna feeling today? ➔ _____
2. What's the matter with her? ➔ _____
3. Is her throat sore? ➔ _____
4. How about her nose? ➔ _____
5. Who is her family doctor? ➔ _____
6. Who is she going to see at the doctor's office? ➔ _____
7. How is she going to go there? ➔ _____
8. Why can't she drive her car today? ➔ _____

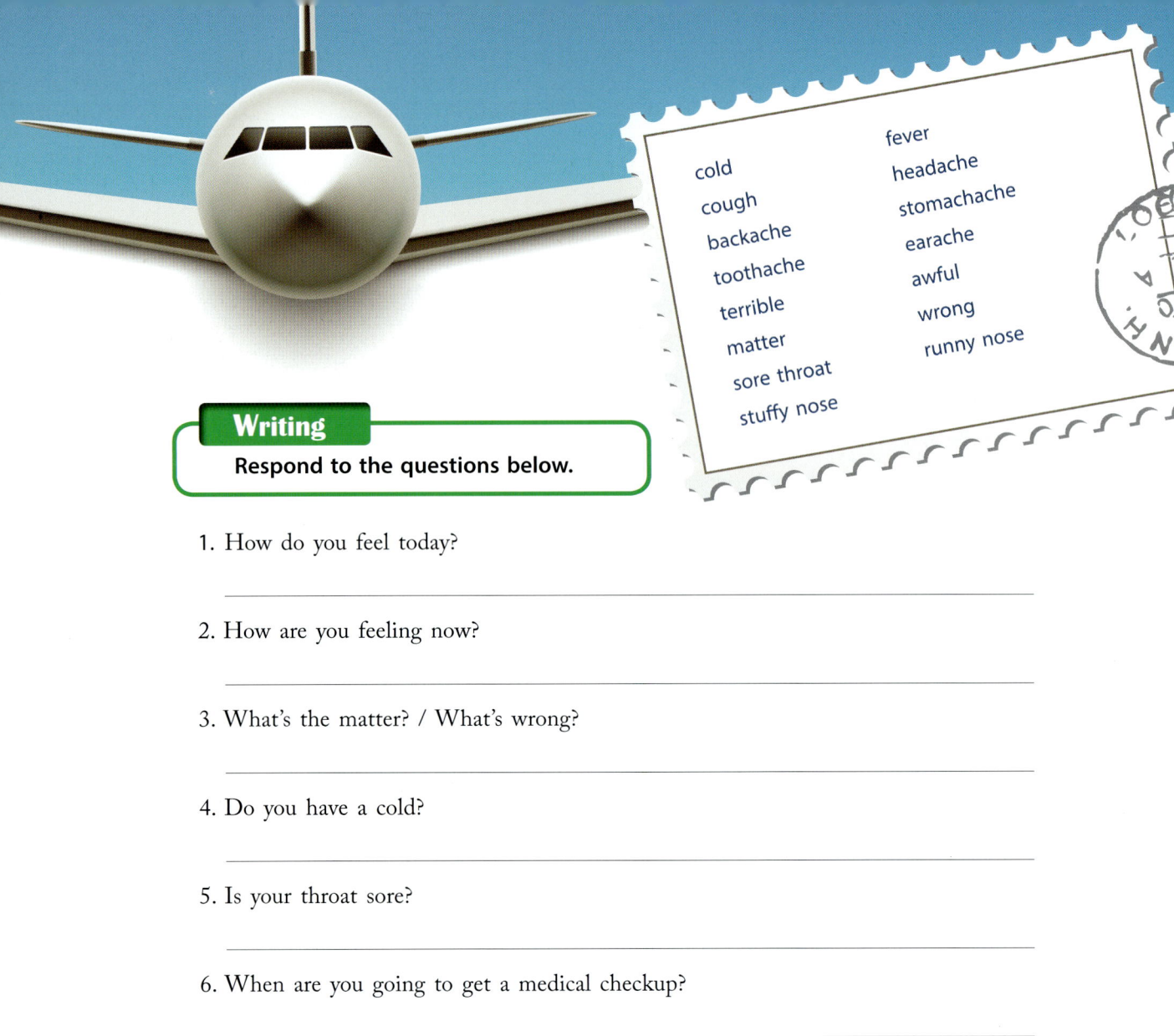

cold	fever
cough	headache
backache	stomachache
toothache	earache
terrible	awful
matter	wrong
sore throat	runny nose
stuffy nose	

Writing

Respond to the questions below.

1. How do you feel today?

2. How are you feeling now?

3. What's the matter? / What's wrong?

4. Do you have a cold?

5. Is your throat sore?

6. When are you going to get a medical checkup?

7. Who's your doctor?

8. How do you get to your doctor's office?

Unit 9 Let's Eat Pizza.

LESSON PLAN

1 Topic
- Suggestion

2 Function
- Suggesting Something and Responding to It
- Agreeing with Somebody

3 Grammar
- Let's + Base verb
- That Sounds + Adjective

1. Let's go outside.
2. Let's not eat junk food.
3. Shall we eat out this evening?
4. Why don't we take a walk for a while?
5. Why don't we go on a diet from today?
6. How about having something delicious now?
7. Do you have time? How about having coffee with me?
8. English is interesting. What do you think?

Unit 9 Let's eat pizza.

1 WORDS & EXPRESSIONS

- attend the meeting
- do one's homework
- go dancing
- go to the swimming pool
- take a walk
- eat out
- go mountain climbing
- go skateboarding
- go to the dentist
- take pictures

2 GRAMMAR

Let's + Base verb		
	Positives	Negatives
Let's + Base verb	Let's eat pizza. = Shall we eat pizza? = Why don't we eat pizza? = How about pizza? / 　How about eating pizza?	Let's not eat pizza.

That Sounds + Adjective
That sounds great[nice, good, awful, bad].

A Put the words in the correct order.

> lunch / take a walk / after / Let's ➡ Let's take a walk after lunch.

1. our / Let's / today / clean / apartment
   ➡ _____

2. not / swimming pool / Let's / go / to / the
   ➡ _____

3. eat / Let's / something hot
   ➡ _____

4. smart / phones / too much / Let's / not use
   ➡ _____

5. healthy / Let's / have / eating habits
   ➡ _____

6. delicious / spaghetti / Let's / this evening / eat
   ➡ _____

7. make a noise / Let's / in / library / not / the
   ➡ _____

B Work with a partner. Rewrite the *Let's* sentences using *Shall we … ?*

> A: Let's eat pizza. ➡ B: Shall we eat pizza?

1. A: Let's go to the movies.
   B: _____
2. A: Let's play tennis today.
   B: _____
3. A: Let's meet in the park at two o'clock.
   B: _____
4. A: Let's finish the work.
   B: _____
5. A: Let's go mountain climbing.
   B: _____
6. A: Let's study together at my house.
   B: _____
7. A: Let's take pictures.
   B: _____

3 CONVERSATION

A Work with a partner. Fill in the blanks and practice the conversation below.

> A: **How about** eating pizza? / **Why don't we** eat pizza?
> B: **That sounds** great. / **That's a good** idea.

1. A: _____ having a drink?
   B: _____ idea.

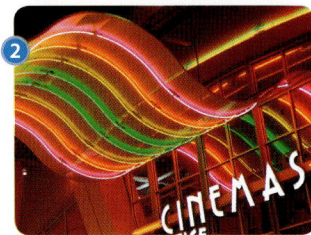

2. A: _____ go to the movies?
   B: _____ idea.

3. A: _____ go to a soccer game?
   B: _____ great.

4. A: _____ having dinner?
   B: _____ great.

5. A: _____ going dancing?
   B: _____ idea.

6. A: _____ go skateboarding?
   B: _____ great.

B Work with a partner. Take turns to ask and answer the questions.

> A: What does Amy think?
> B: She agrees.

1. A: What _____ you think?
   B: _____

2. A: What _____ your children think?
   B: _____

3. A: What _____ Billy think?
   B: _____

4. A: What _____ you and Wilson think?
   B: _____

5. A: What _____ Natalie think?
   B: _____

6. A: What _____ her parents think?
   B: _____

C Work with a partner. Practice the conversation using the words below.

> A: Let's go to Janet's party.
> B: I'm sorry. I can't. I have to <u>fix my car</u>.

1. work
2. go to the doctor
3. do my homework
4. wash my clothes
5. go to the dentist
6. attend the meeting

Unit 9 77

D Listen and practice.

A: I'm hungry. Let's eat something. What do you think?
B: Good idea. Why don't we go to Pizza Planet?
A: That sounds great. Their pizza is fantastic.
B: I agree.

▶ Work with a partner. Practice the conversation using the words below.

A: I'm _____. Let's _____. What do you think?
B: Good idea. Why don't we go to _____?
A: That sounds _____. Their _____ is fantastic.
B: I agree.

1. thirsty / drink something
   Johnson's
   nice / milk shake

2. hot / have something cold
   Orange King
   wonderful / ice cream

3. starving / eat something
   Italian Life
   terrific / spaghetti

4. cold / have something hot
   Lemon Tree
   good / French onion soup

▶ Using these models, create dialogs with a partner.

E Take turns to round the class. One student suggests something and the rest of the classmates answer like the conversation below.

A: Let's go to the movies together after class.
B: Sounds great. / That's a good idea. / That's not a good idea. / We're sorry. We can't.

78 English Fly High | Boarding

Out to the world with Mr. Moon!

Reading & Writing
Read the passage below and correct the wrong sentences.

Do you want to be healthy? Let's go on a diet. How about drinking a glass of water instead of soda and sugary juice? Let's drink more than 8 glasses of water a day. Let's not eat any fried foods such as French fries or burgers. Why don't we eat salmon, beans, tofu, and eggs? They're rich in protein. Let's have colorful vegetables and fruits such as tomatoes, paprika, and blueberries. They're rich in vitamins, fiber, and minerals. Let's not eat any desserts with cream, butter, or chocolate. Eating habits are really important. Let's have healthy eating habits.

1. Soda and sugary juice are good for your health.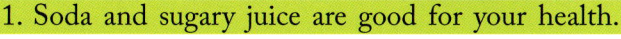
2. French fries and burgers aren't fried foods.
3. Eggs are rich in fiber.
4. Salmon is rich in vitamins.
5. Colorful vegetables are rich in protein.
6. Desserts with cream are helpful to your health.
7. Eating habits aren't really important.

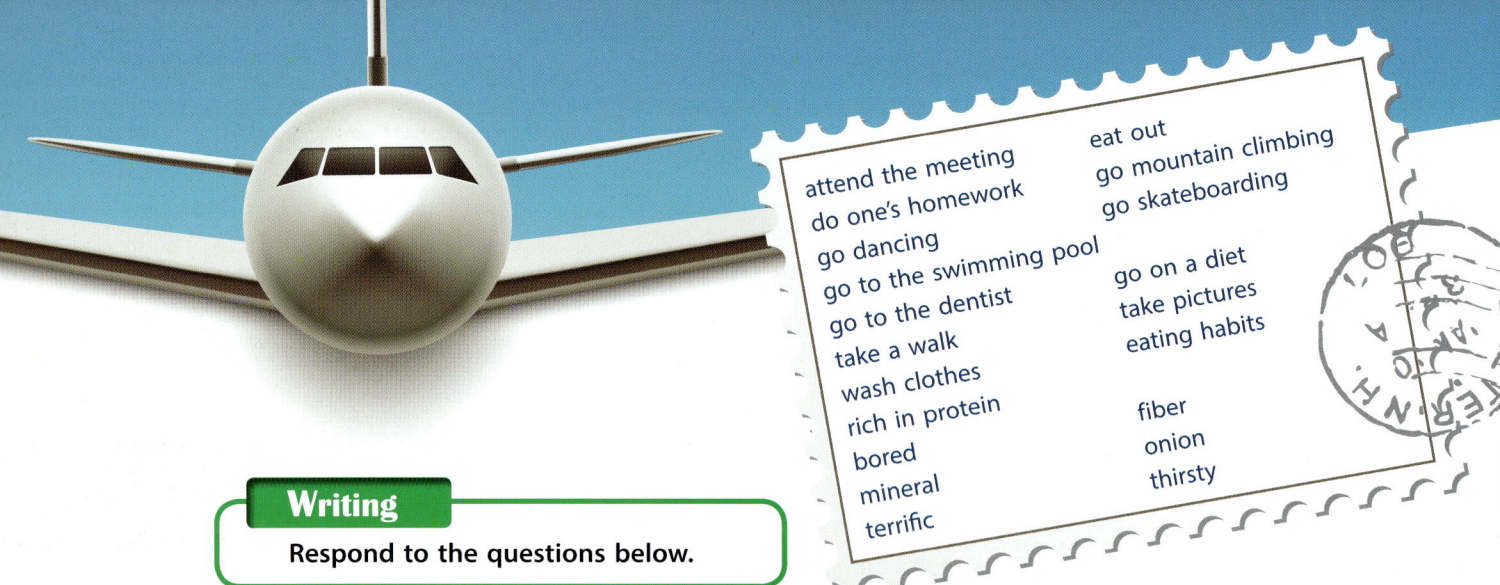

attend the meeting
do one's homework
go dancing
go to the swimming pool
go to the dentist
take a walk
wash clothes
rich in protein
bored
mineral
terrific
eat out
go mountain climbing
go skateboarding
go on a diet
take pictures
eating habits
fiber
onion
thirsty

Writing

Respond to the questions below.

1. Let's go outside.

2. Let's not eat junk food.

3. Shall we eat out this evening?

4. Why don't we take a walk for a while?

5. Why don't we go on a diet from today?

6. How about having something delicious now?

7. Do you have time? How about having coffee with me?

8. English is interesting. What do you think?

Unit 10 I Was at Home Yesterday.

LESSON PLAN

1) Topic
- Past Actions and Activities

2) Function
- Asking and Answering Questions about the Past
- Describing Physical States and Emotions

3) Grammar
- Past Tense of Be verb (Was / Were)
- Be Busy ~ing

1. Were you at home yesterday?
2. Where were you yesterday?
3. Why were you there?
4. Were you on time for school[work] yesterday?
5. Was it hot yesterday?
6. Were you tired or energetic last week?
7. Was lunch delicious this afternoon?
8. Was your father handsome?

Unit 10 I was at home yesterday.

1 WORDS & EXPRESSIONS

1. short - tall
2. hungry - full
3. tired - energetic
4. delicious - terrible
5. hot - cool

- in the park
- at the airport
- at school
- at the office
- at the church
- at home
- in the playground
- at the gym
- in the library
- at the mall
- at the party
- at the restaurant
- at the beach
- at the hospital
- at work

2 GRAMMAR

Past Tense of Be verb (Was/Were)	
Positives	Negatives
I was	I wasn't
You were	You weren't
He/She/It was	He/She/It wasn't
We were	We weren't
They were	They weren't
Questions	Short Answers
Was I?	Yes, you were. / No, you weren't.
Were you?	Yes, I was. / No, I wasn't.
Was he/she/it?	Yes, he/she/it was. / No, he/she/it wasn't.
Were we?	Yes, we were. / No, we weren't.
Were they?	Yes they were. / No, they weren't.

Be Busy ~ing
I was busy studying in the library.

A Rewrite the sentences using the past simple of *be verb*.

1. I'm happy. ➔ _____

2. My sister is angry with me. ➔ _____

3. We're not children anymore. ➔ _____

4. Mary's dog is very friendly. ➔ _____

5. Dan is tall and strong. ➔ _____

6. Ronald is a high school teacher. ➔ _____

7. They are busy preparing for a party. ➔ _____

B Work with a partner. Fill in the blanks to make questions and answers.

> A: **Was** Jill in the park yesterday?
> B: Yes, **she was**. **She was** in the park all day long. / No, **she wasn't**. **She was** at home.

1. A: _____ Kevin short three years ago?
   B: Yes, _____. _____ a very small boy.

2. A: _____ you a baseball player?
   B: No, _____. _____ a football player.

3. A: _____ you and your boyfriend at the party?
   B: No, _____. _____ at the airport.

4. A: _____ Laura busy last week?
   B: Yes, _____. _____ very busy.

5. A: _____ his father a famous actor?
   B: No, _____. _____ a famous singer.

6. A: _____ Mr. Joel rich?
   B: Yes, _____. _____ very rich.

7. A: _____ the Korean people diligent?
   B: Yes, _____. _____ very diligent.

3 CONVERSATION

A Work with a partner. Fill in the blanks and practice the conversation below.

A: Sam **was** hungry last night.
B: **He is** full now.

A: Ricky _____ twenty years old last year.
B: _____ twenty one years old now.

A: Molly and I _____ at school this morning.
B: _____ at home now.

A: My brother _____ tired yesterday.
B: _____ energetic now.

A: Robin and his friends _____ students 6 years ago.
B: _____ doctors now.

A: Mrs. Kim _____ beautiful in her twenties.
B: _____ very old now.

A: There _____ a lot of children in the playground this morning.
B: There _____ no children in the playground now.

B Work with a partner. Fill in the blanks and practice the conversation below.

> A: Were you at the restaurant yesterday?
> B: Yes, I was. I was busy meeting with somebody.

1. **prepare the presentation**
   A: _____ Hank at the office yesterday?
   B: Yes, _____. _____ busy _____.

2. **do her homework**
   A: _____ your sister at the library yesterday?
   B: Yes, _____. _____ busy _____.

3. **clean out the drawer**
   A: _____ Monica at home yesterday?
   B: Yes, _____. _____ busy _____.

4. **play basketball**
   A: _____ Ralph and Bobby at the gym yesterday?
   B: Yes, _____. _____ busy _____.

5. **work a part-time job**
   A: _____ you at the cafeteria yesterday?
   B: Yes, _____. _____ busy _____.

6. **get a medical check up**
   A: _____ Ariel and her grandmother at the hospital yesterday?
   B: Yes, _____. _____ busy _____.

C Work with a partner. Take turns to ask and answer the questions.

> A: Were you happy yesterday?
> B: No, I wasn't. I was sad.

1. Steven / at home this morning / at work
2. it / hot yesterday / cool
3. the food / delicious at the restaurant / terrible
4. your son / late for school / on time
5. Thelma and her husband / at work / on vacation
6. Lewis / a teacher / an engineer

D Listen and practice. 🎧 19

A: Where were you yesterday?
B: I was in the library all day long.
A: Why were you there?
B: I was busy doing my homework.

▶ Work with a partner. Practice the conversation using the words below.

> A: Where _____ yesterday?
> B: _____ all day long.
> A: Why _____ there?
> B: _____ busy _____.

1. Gloria
   at the gym
   practicing yoga

2. Tom and Lisa
   at the church
   preparing for the wedding

3. your mother
   at home
   cooking for a birthday party

4. Frank
   at the office
   answering phone calls

▶ Using these models, create dialogs with a partner.

E Work in groups. Look at the pictures. What differences can you see? Take turns to guess them using the present and the past of be verb like below.

Yesterday

Today

> *Yesterday **there were** three clouds. Today **there are** two clouds.*

86 English Fly High | Boarding

Out to the world with Mr. Moon!

Reading & Writing
Read the passage below and answer the questions. [20]

Bill wasn't at home last week. He was on vacation. Bill and his brother Jessie were at the beach. Their dog Snoopy and all their friends were with them, too. His sister Helen wasn't there. She was at her aunt's house. She was spending time with her cousins there. Bill's parents were at home. Actually they were very happy because the house was very quiet. Their neighbors were also happy because Snoopy wasn't there. He always barks, chases cats, and makes a lot of noise. Everybody was happy and satisfied last week.

1. Where were Bill and his brother last week? ➔ _____
2. Who were with them? ➔ _____
3. Where was Helen? ➔ _____
4. Where were Bill's parents? ➔ _____
5. Why were his parents happy? ➔ _____
6. Why were their neighbors happy? ➔ _____
7. What does Snoopy always do? ➔ _____

Unit 10 87

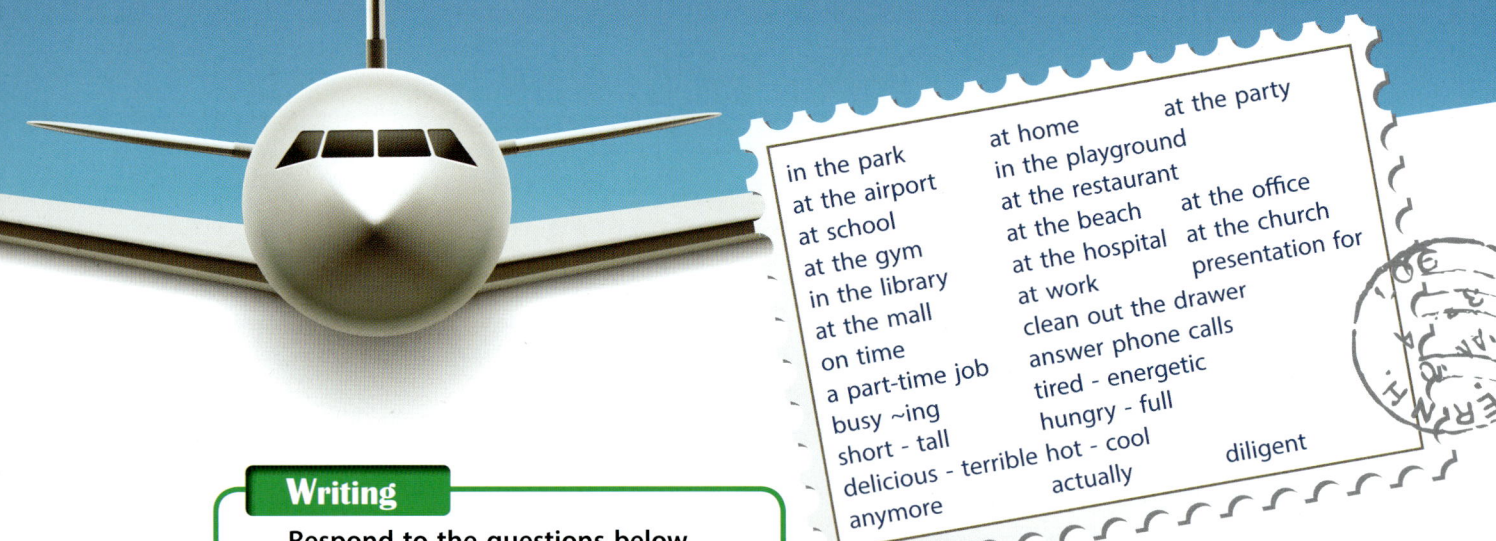

Writing

Respond to the questions below.

1. Were you at home yesterday?
   _____

2. Where were you yesterday?
   _____

3. Why were you there?
   _____

4. Were you on time for school[work] yesterday?
   _____

5. Was it hot yesterday?
   _____

6. Were you tired or energetic last week?
   _____

7. Was lunch delicious this afternoon?
   _____

8. Was your father handsome?
   _____

Answers

Unit 1 How's everything?

❷ GRAMMAR

A 1. am 2. are 3. is 4. is 5. are 6. Are 7. are

B 1. Is Mr. Johnson a professor?
2. Are all the workers out for lunch now?
3. Is it sunny and hot outside?
4. Is my dog very smart?
5. Are Sheena and her friends at the beach?
6. Is there a big supermarket near my house?
7. Is Nina your best friend?

❸ CONVERSATION

A 1. are / 're 2. is / 's 3. are / 're 4. are / 're 5. is / 's 6. is / 's

B 1. is / She's doing terrible.
3. is / It's doing very well.
5. is / He's doing good.
2. are / They're doing great.
4. are / We're doing okay.
6. is / She's doing pretty good.

C 1. A: How's work going?
   B: Nothing much.
3. A: How's the new job?
   B: Not too bad.
5. A: How's your vacation going?
   B: Couldn't be worse.
2. A: How's your diet going?
   B: Not so well.
4. A: How's the English class going?
   B: Couldn't be better.

D 1. A: Hi, Amy. How's work going?
   B: Pretty good, thanks. How are your brothers?
   A: They're great, too. See you again.
   B: Take care.

3. A: Hi, Kevin. How're your parents?
   B: Great, thanks. How are your children?
   A: They're okay, too. See you around.
   B: Take care.

5. A: Hi, Laura. How're your fingers?
   B: Better, thanks. How are you and your roommates?
   A: We're fine, too. See you tomorrow.
   B: Take care.

2. A: Hi, Adam. How're you doing?
   B: Not so bad, thanks. How are Max and James?
   A: They're good, too. See you soon.
   B: Take care.

4. A: Hi, Lucy. How's school going?
   B: Good, thanks. How are you and your dog?
   A: We're great, too. See you next time.
   B: Take care.

Out to the world with Mr. Moon

Reading & Writing

1. Tina has a photo of her **sister**.
2. Tina has a **sister** called Tammy.
3. Ben **can** look at the photo.
4. Tammy is a **singer**.
5. Tammy is in **Las Vegas**.
6. Tammy plays the **guitar**.
7. Tammy **is** Tina's good friend.

Unit 2 Please call me Bob.

❷ GRAMMAR

A 1. them   2. him   3. her   4. it   5. He   6. She   7. me

B 1. She is from London.
2. It is Kenny.
3. Don is talking to her.
4. Where is he from?
5. We are all tall.
6. I want to drink it.
7. They are very friendly.

❸ CONVERSATION

A 1. His name is
2. His name is
3. Their names are
4. Her name is
5. Their names are

B 1. Where is / He's
2. Where is / She's
3. Where are / They're
4. Where are / We're
5. Where is / She's
6. Where is / He's

D 1. A: I'm Aaron. I'm from Manhattan, America.
B: My name is Samantha Grant. Please call me Sam.
A: Are you from around here, Sam?
B: Yes, right here in Liverpool.

2. A: I'm Ben. I'm from Sydney, Australia.
B: My name is Victoria King. Please call me Vicky.
A: Are you from around here, Vicky?
B: Yes, right here in Toronto.

3. A: I'm Gina. I'm from Rome, Italy.
B: My name is Christopher Reeve. Please call me Chris.
A: Are you from around here, Chris?
B: Yes, right here in Texas.

4. A: I'm Pierre. I'm from Paris, France.
B: My name is Pamela Anderson. Please call me Pam.
A: Are you from around here, Pam?
B: Yes, right here in Miami.

5. A: I'm Yukki. I'm from Hiroshima, Japan.
B: My name is Melvin Kate. Please call me Mel.
A: Are you from around here, Mel?
B: Yes, right here in California.

Out to the world with Mr. Moon
Reading & Writing

1. Her name(It) is Julie Devoir.
2. She is thirty years old.
3. She's from Quebec, Canada.
4. She wants to help her students with French.
5. Her address(It) is 456 Main Street, Riverside, Philadelphia.
6. Her phone number(It) is 010-111-2345.
7. Her e-mail address(It) is French30@school.com.

Unit 3 I like going camping.

❷ GRAMMAR

A
1. like / don't like
3. likes / doesn't like
5. like / don't like
7. like / don't like

2. likes / doesn't like
4. like / don't like
6. likes / doesn't like

B
1. Mickey likes playing badminton.
2. My friends like playing basketball.
3. The Jones family likes playing baseball.
4. Sam likes playing the guitar.
5. They like playing the piano.
6. Her parents like playing cards.
7. We like playing the game.

❸ CONVERSATION

A
1. I don't like cooking spaghetti
2. he likes swimming
3. he likes riding a bicycle
4. she doesn't like washing the dishes
5. they like going camping
6. he doesn't like dancing at the club

B
1. Do / I do / I love animals.
2. Does / she doesn't / She hates writing letters.
3. Does / he does / He likes cheese.
4. Do / they don't / They hate going shopping.
5. Do / I do / I like learning English.
6. Does / she doesn't / She hates meat.

D
1. A: I like baseball. What's your favorite sport?
   B: My favorite sport is soccer.
   A: Why?
   B: I like watching it and soccer players are handsome.

3. A: I like history. What's your favorite subject?
   B: My favorite subject is English.
   A: Why?
   B: I like speaking English and the teacher is handsome.

5. A: I like boxing. What's your favorite sport?
   B: My favorite sport is body building.
   A: Why?
   B: I like exercising and body builders are handsome.

2. A: I like classical music. What's your favorite music?
   B: My favorite music is rock music.
   A: Why?
   B: I like listening to it and rock singers are handsome.

4. A: I like horror movies. What's your favorite movie?
   B: My favorite movie is a musical movie.
   A: Why?
   B: I like music and actors are handsome.

Out to the world with Mr. Moon

Reading & Writing

1. The dog's name is **Sam**.
2. Sam sleeps **in the front yard**.
3. He gets up very **early**.
4. He **likes** chasing cats.
5. He **makes a lot of noise**.
6. He really likes **playing with a ball**.
7. He **hates** taking a bath.

Unit 4 Is it snowing?

❷ GRAMMAR

A 1. yours 2. hers 3. mine 4. ours 5. his 6. theirs 7. ours

B 1. It's raining a lot now
3. He's drinking coffee now
5. I'm writing a diary now
7. They're delivering the newspaper now
2. She's brushing her teeth now
4. We're watching TV now
6. It's snowing now

❸ CONVERSATION

A 1. it's not raining / It's cloudy
3. it's not raining / It's windy
5. it's not raining / It's freezing
2. it's not raining / It's snowing
4. it's not raining / It's fine
6. it's not raining / It's wonderful

B 1. the weather like / It's warm.
3. the weather like / It's cool.
5. the weather like / It's cold.
2. the weather like / It's hot.
4. the weather / It's pouring.
6. the weather / It's chilly.

C 1. A: Is he walking?
　　B: No, he's running.
3. A: Are they swimming?
　　B: No, they're taking a rest.
5. A: Is she crying?
　　B: No, she's laughing.
2. A: Is she sleeping?
　　B: No, she's taking a shower.
4. A: Are you having a good time?
　　B: No, I'm having a terrible time.
6. A: Is he shouting?
　　B: No, he's singing.

D 1. A: It's snowing today.
　　B: I need big gloves. Mine are too small. Can I borrow yours?
　　A: Of course but mine are not so big.
　　B: That's okay. Thanks a lot.

2. A: It's pouring today.
　　B: I need big rain boots. Mine are too small. Can I borrow yours?
　　A: Of course but mine are not so big.
　　B: That's okay. Thanks a lot.

3. A: It's storming today.
　　B: I need a big raincoat. Mine is too small. Can I borrow yours?
　　A: Of course but mine is not so big.
　　B: That's okay. Thanks a lot.

4. A: It's freezing today.
　　B: I need a big scarf. Mine is too small. Can I borrow yours?
　　A: Of course but mine is not so big.
　　B: That's okay. Thanks a lot.

Out to the world with Mr. Moon
Reading & Writing

1. She's at a hotel in Michigan.
3. It's freezing and snowing.
5. She's sitting on the sofa and watching movies on TV.
7. She's in Florida.
2. The weather isn't good in Michigan.
4. No, she can't.
6. No, she's having a terrible time.

Unit 5 I'm going to visit the old palace.

❷ GRAMMAR

A
1. am going to
2. is going to
3. is going to
4. is going to
5. are going to
6. are going to
7. is going to

B
1. He's going to break it.
2. He's going to borrow some money.
3. I'm going to be late for school.
4. She's going to cry.
5. I'm going to give it to my friend.
6. We're going to go to the bathroom.
7. You're going to pass the examination.

❸ CONVERSATION

A
1. are / I'm going to come home
2. are / They're going to get together
3. are / We're going to eat dinner
4. is / It's going to leave
5. is / It's going to arrive
6. are / They're going to have a party

B
1. hot / It's going to be cool.
2. sunny / It's going to be snowy.
3. cloudy / It's going to be sunny.
4. warm / It's going to be cold.
5. chilly / It's going to be warm.
6. rainy / It's going to be fine.

C
1. A: What is Dick going to do this weekend?
   B: He's going to visit an old palace.
2. A: What are you and your family going to do this weekend?
   B: We're going to go camping.
3. A: What are Emma and Daniel going to do this weekend?
   B: They're going to go to the concert.
4. A: What is Annette going to do this weekend?
   B: She's going to do some grocery shopping.
5. A: What are you going to do this weekend?
   B: I'm going to move out.
6. A: What are your parents going to do this weekend?
   B: They're going to clean the garage.

D
1. A: Hi, Betty! Where are you going?
   B: I'm going to the park. I'm going to take a walk before 7 o'clock. What time is it?
   A: It's 6:30 already.
   B: Oops! I'm sorry, but I have to leave now. See you later.
2. A: Hi, Warren! Where are you going?
   B: I'm going to the post office. I'm going to send the parcel by 5 o'clock. What time is it?
   A: It's 4:45 already.
   B: Oops! I'm sorry, but I have to leave now. See you later.
3. A: Hi, Kevin! Where are you going?
   B: I'm going to the restaurant. I'm going to have lunch with somebody at 1 o'clock. What time is it?
   A: It's 12:55 already.
   B: Oops! I'm sorry, but I have to leave now. See you later.
4. A: Hi, Max! Where are you going?
   B: I'm going to the supermarket. I'm going to buy some bananas before 4 o'clock. What time is it?
   A: It's 3:40 already.
   B: Oops! I'm sorry, but I have to leave now. See you later.

Out to the world with Mr. Moon
Reading & Writing

1. She's looking for the student cafeteria.
2. He's going to take Cindy to the student cafeteria.
3. Her family name is Last.
4. He's from Boston.
5. She's from Kansas.
6. He's going to eat lunch there.
7. Yes, she's going to join Max.

Unit 6 Don't be nervous.

2 GRAMMAR

A 1. want 2. wants 3. to 4. Does 5. wants 6. Do 7. to

B 1. Don't sit down.
2. Go to sleep.
3. Don't say hello to her.
4. Shut the window.
5. Don't watch TV all day long.
6. Always smile.
7. Don't get up late.

3 CONVERSATION

A 1. Don't be angry / Just eat something.
2. Don't be embarrassed / Just take it easy.
3. Don't be nervous / Just make yourself at home.
4. Don't blush / Just say hello to him.
5. Don't cry / Just cheer up.

B 1. Is John the one with black hair? / he has black hair
2. Is Bridget the one with blue eyes? / she has blue eyes
3. Are Tom's sisters the ones with curly hair? / they have curly hair
4. Is Karen the one with straight hair? / she has straight hair
5. Are his children the ones with red hair? / they have red hair
6. Is Brad the one with brown eyes? / he has brown eyes

C 1. A: How do I look?
B: You look great.

2. A: How does Andy look?
B: He looks cute.

3. A: How do his sisters look?
B: They look wonderful.

4. A: How does Abigail look?
B: She looks gorgeous.

5. A: How does Clark look?
B: He looks handsome.

6. A: How does Daisy look?
B: She looks beautiful.

D 1. A: Do you see the short girl with blue skirt? I like her.
B: The one with black hair? She looks cute. Say hello to her.
A: I want to but I can't. I'm so shy.
B: Don't be shy. Be brave!

2. A: Do you see the thin girl with white skirt? I like her.
B: The one with curly hair? She looks pretty. Say hello to her.
A: I want to but I can't. I'm so embarrassed.
B: Don't be embarrassed. Be brave!

3. A: Do you see the slender girl with pink blouse? I like her.
B: The one with straight hair? She looks nice. Say hello to her.
A: I want to but I can't. I'm so scared.
B: Don't be scared. Be brave!

4. A: Do you see the chubby girl with brown sweater? I like her.
B: The one with long hair? She looks wonderful. Say hello to her.
A: I want to but I can't. I blush.
B: Don't blush. Be brave!

5. A: Do you see the slim girl with orange shorts? I like her.
B: The one with short hair? She looks great. Say hello to her.
A: I want to but I can't. I panic.
B: Don't panic. Be brave!

Out to the world with Mr. Moon
Reading & Writing

1. Sally **wants** to be slim and look gorgeous.
2. She **is** trying hard for her health.
3. She **doesn't** skip breakfast.
4. She **doesn't** like fast food.
5. She takes **stairs** instead of **elevators**.
6. She **doesn't** want to eat junk food.
7. She likes drinking **green tea**.

Unit 7 Where can I find the gas station?

2 GRAMMAR

A
1. Is there a flower shop around here?
2. Are there jewelry stores near here?
3. Is there a library on First Avenue?
4. Are there convenience stores in this area?
5. Is there a shopping mall on Maple Street?
6. Are there pay phones in this neighborhood?
7. Is there a subway station on the corner?

B
1. Where can I find the bank?
2. Where can I find the post office?
3. Where can I find the book stores?
4. Where can I find the bus stop?
5. Where can I find the convenience stores?
6. Where can I find the hospital?
7. Where can I find the department store?

3 CONVERSATION

A
1. is / It's on
2. are / They're at
3. is / It's on
4. are / They're on
5. is / It's at
6. are / They're on

D
1. A: How can I get to the hospital?
   B: Do you see that building?
   A: Do you mean the white new one?
   B: That's the library. And the hospital is in front of it. You can't miss it.

2. A: Where is the hospital?
   B: Do you see that building?
   A: Do you mean the old wooden one?
   B: That's the library. And the hospital is behind it. You can't miss it.

3. A: Can you tell me the way to the hospital?
   B: Do you see that building?
   A: Do you mean the new concrete one?
   B: That's the library. And the hospital is across from it. You can't miss it.

4. A: Can you show me the way to the hospital?
   B: Do you see that building?
   A: Do you mean the old small one?
   B: That's the library. And the hospital is opposite to it. You can't miss it.

Out to the world with Mr. Moon
Reading & Writing

1. **Donald** is looking for the movie theater.
2. Joseph **doesn't know** where the movie theater is. (or **Lucy** knows where the movie theater is.)
3. Lucy is **Joseph's** friend.
4. The movie theater is **on Main Street** next to the library.
5. The library is **across from** the hospital.
6. Lucy **isn't** angry at Donald.
7. The big white building on Main Street is **the hospital**.

Unit 8　I have a headache.

❷ GRAMMAR

A 1. Where　2. What　3. How　4. Why　5. When　6. Who　7. Why

B 1. It's　2. I'm　3. I get　4. She's　5. I'm　6. He feels　7. they're

❸ CONVERSATION

A
1. I feel
2. She feels
3. He's feeling
4. They feel
5. They're feeling
6. He's feeling

B
1. She has a fever.
2. She has a headache.
3. He has a runny nose.
4. I have an earache.
5. He has a stuffy nose.
6. We have a cough.

D
1. A: How do you feel?
   B: Not so well.
   A: What's the matter?
   B: I have a headache.
   A: I'm sorry to hear that.

3. A: How do you feel?
   B: Not so great.
   A: What's the matter?
   B: I have a fever.
   A: I'm sorry to hear that.

5. A: How do you feel?
   B: Not so good.
   A: What's the matter?
   B: I have a sore throat.
   A: I'm sorry to hear that.

2. A: How do you feel?
   B: I don't feel good.
   A: What's wrong?
   B: I have a backache.
   A: That's too bad.

4. A: How do you feel?
   B: I don't feel well.
   A: What's wrong?
   B: I have a toothache.
   A: That's too bad.

Out to the world with Mr. Moon
Reading & Writing

1. She's not feeling well.
2. She has a fever and headache.
3. Yes, her throat is sore.
4. Her nose is runny all day long.
5. Her family doctor is Mr. Brown.
6. She's going to see Dr. Bell there.
7. She's going to go there by taxi.
8. Because she's very sick.

Unit 9 Let's eat pizza.

2 GRAMMAR

A
1. Let's clean our apartment today.
2. Let's not go to the swimming pool.
3. Let's eat something hot.
4. Let's not use smart phones too much.
5. Let's have healthy eating habits.
6. Let's eat delicious spaghetti this evening.
7. Let's not make a noise in the library.

B
1. Shall we go to the movies?
2. Shall we play tennis today?
3. Shall we meet in the park at two o'clock?
4. Shall we finish the work?
5. Shall we go mountain climbing?
6. Shall we study together at my house?
7. Shall we take pictures?

3 CONVERSATION

A
1. How about / That's a good
2. Why don't we / That's a good
3. Why don't we / That sounds
4. How about / That sounds
5. How about / That's a good
6. Why don't we / That sounds

B
1. do / I agree.
2. do / They agree.
3. does / He agrees.
4. do / We agree.
5. does / She agrees.
6. do / They agree.

D
1. A: I'm thirsty. Let's drink something. What do you think?
   B: Good idea. Why don't we go to Johnson's?
   A: That sounds nice. Their milk shake is fantastic.
   B: I agree.

2. A: I'm hot. Let's have something cold. What do you think?
   B: Good idea. Why don't we go to Orange King?
   A: That sounds wonderful. Their ice cream is fantastic.
   B: I agree.

3. A: I'm starving. Let's eat something. What do you think?
   B: Good idea. Why don't we go to Italian Life?
   A: That sounds terrific. Their spaghetti is fantastic.
   B : I agree.

4. A: I'm cold. Let's have something hot. What do you think?
   B: Good idea. Why don't we go to Lemon Tree?
   A: That sounds good. Their French onion soup is fantastic.
   B : I agree.

Out to the world with Mr. Moon

Reading & Writing

1. Soda and sugary juice **aren't** good for your health.
2. French fries and burgers **are** fried foods.
3. Eggs **aren't** rich in fiber. (or Eggs are rich in **protein**.)
4. Salmon **isn't** rich in vitamins. (or Salmon is rich in **protein**.)
5. Colorful vegetables **aren't** rich in protein. (or Colorful vegetables are rich in **vitamins, fiber, and minerals**.)
6. Desserts with cream **aren't** helpful to your health.
7. Eating habits **are** really important.

Unit 10 I was at home yesterday.

❷ GRAMMAR

A
1. I was happy.
2. My sister was angry with me.
3. We weren't children anymore.
4. Mary's dog was very friendly.
5. Dan was tall and strong.
6. Ronald was a high school teacher.
7. They were busy preparing for a party.

B
1. Was / he was / He was
2. Were / I wasn't / I was
3. Were / we weren't / We were
4. Was / she was / She was
5. Was / he wasn't / He was
6. Was / he was / He was
7. Were / they were / They were

❸ CONVERSATION

A
1. was / He is
2. were / We are
3. was / He is
4. were / They are
5. was / She is
6. were / are

B
1. Was / he was / He was / preparing the presentation
2. Was / she was / She was / doing her homework
3. Was / she was / She was / cleaning out the drawer
4. Were / they were / They were / playing basketball
5. Were / I was / I was / working a part-time job
6. Were / they were / They were / getting a medical check up

C
1. A: Was Steven at home this morning?
   B: No, he wasn't. He was at work.
2. A: Was it hot yesterday?
   B: No, it wasn't. It was cool.
3. A: Was the food delicious at the restaurant?
   B: No, it wasn't. It was terrible.
4. A: Was your son late for school?
   B: No, he wasn't. He was on time.
5. A: Were Thelma and her husband at work?
   B: No, they weren't. They were on vacation.
6. A: Was Lewis a teacher?
   B: No, he wasn't. He was an engineer.

D
1. A: Where was Gloria yesterday?
   B: She was at the gym all day long.
   A: Why was she there?
   B: She was busy practicing yoga.
2. A: Where were Tom and Lisa yesterday?
   B: They were at the church all day long.
   A: Why were they there?
   B: They were busy preparing for the wedding.
3. A: Where was your mother yesterday?
   B: She was at home all day long.
   A: Why was she there?
   B: She was busy cooking for a birthday party.
4. A: Where was Frank yesterday?
   B: He was at the office all day long.
   A: Why was he there?
   B: He was busy answering phone calls.

Out to the world with Mr. Moon
Reading & Writing

1. They were at the beach.
2. Their dog Snoopy and all their friends were with them.
3. She was at her aunt's house.
4. They were at home.
5. Because the house was very quiet.
6. Because Snoopy wasn't there.
7. He always barks, chases cats, and makes a lot of noise.

Appendixes

Grammar Summary

Unit 1

Be verbs							
Statements		**Questions**		**Answers**			
I am		Am I			you are.		you are not.
You are		Are you			I am.		I am not.
He/She/It is	okay.	Is he/she/it	okay?	Yes,	he/she/it is.	No,	he/she/it is not.
We are		Are we			we are.		we are not.
They are		Are they			they are.		they are not.

Contractions	
I am = I'm	I am not = I'm not
You are = You're	You are not = You aren't
He is = He's	He is not = He isn't
She is = She's	She is not = She isn't
It is = It's	It is not = It isn't
We are = We're	We are not = We aren't
They are = They're	They are not = They aren't

Unit 2

Pronouns (Subject / Object), Possessive Adjectives			
Subjects	**Objects**	**Possessive Adjectives + Noun**	
I	me	my	
you	you	your	
he	him	his	
she	her	her	name
it	it	its	
we	us	our	
they	them	their	

Possessive of Nouns (Noun + 's)	Tom's glasses the boy's brother birds' song

Unit 3

Simple Present

Statements	WH-Questions
I like history.	What subject do you like?
You like history.	What subject do I like?
He/She likes history.	What subject does he/she like?
We like history.	What subject do we like?
They like history.	What subject do they like?

Questions	Answers	
Do I like history?	Yes, you do.	No, you don't.
Do you like history?	Yes, I do.	No, I don't.
Does he/she like history?	Yes, he/she does.	No, he/she doesn't.
Do we like history?	Yes, we do.	No, we don't.
Do they like history?	Yes, they do.	No, they don't.

- The verb after he, she, it (3rd person singular) has a final –s.

Like[Love, Hate] + Noun / ~ing

I like[love, hate] books. / I like[love, hate] reading books.

Unit 4

Present Continuous / Possessive Pronouns

Statements		Questions		Possessive Pronouns
I am		Am I		mine
You are		Are you		yours
He is		Is he		his
She is	eating.	Is she	eating?	hers
We are		Are we		ours
They are		Are they		theirs

Unit 5

Future Tense: Be Going to + Verb

Subject + Be Going to + Verb		Questions	
I am		Am I	
You are		Are you	
He/She is	going to visit the old palace.	Is he/she	going to visit the old palace?
We are		Are we	
They are		Are they	

Answers				WH-Questions			
Yes,	you are. I am. he is. she is. we are. they are.	No,	you aren't. I'm not. he isn't. she isn't. we aren't. they aren't.	What	am I are you is he is she are we are they		going to do?

Unit 6

Imperatives: (Subject) Verb + Modifier

	Positives	Negatives
(You)	Come here. Be quiet.	Don't come here. Don't be quiet.

Want to + Base verb

Positives		Negatives		Questions			
I You We They	want to study abroad.	I You We They	don't want to study abroad.	Do	I you we they	want to study abroad?	
He She	wants to study abroad.	He She	doesn't want to study abroad.	Does	he she	want to study abroad?	

Colors

white   yellow   orange   pink   red   green   blue   purple   gray   black

Unit 7

Prepositions of Location	
on + (name of the street)	at + (address number)
The library is on Main Street.	My office is at 123 Maple Street.
next to, across from(opposite), in front of, behind, between ~ and ~	
The bank is next to[across from, in front of, behind] the library. The bank is between the library and the bakery.	
Imperatives: (Subject) Verb + Modifier	
(You) Turn right. / (You) Turn left. Go along[up, down, straight ahead].	

Asking for Directions	
Where is the gas station? Where can I find the gas station? How can I get to the gas station? Can you tell me the way to the gas station? Can you show me the way to the gas station? Is there a gas station around here?	Go up First Avenue to Main Street. Turn right and go straight ahead to Second Avenue. The gas station is on the right.

Unit 8

WH-Questions: What, Who, Where, When, Why, How			
Questions	Verbs	Subjects	Verbs
What	is	your name?	
Who	are	you?	
Where	are	you?	
When	is	your birthday?	
What	do	you	do?
Where	does	he	live?
When	does	she	go to bed?
Why	do	they	study?
How	do	you	feel?

Questions	Verbs	Subjects	Verbs
What	are	you	doing?
Who	is	he	watching?
Where	are	you	going?
When	is	she	going to marry?
Why	are	you	crying?
How	are	you	feeling?

Sickness
I/You/We/They have a cold[fever, cough, headache, toothache, etc.].   He/She has a cold[fever, cough, headache, toothache, etc.].

Grammar Summary 105

Unit 9

	Let's + Base verb	
	Positives	**Negatives**
Let's + Base verb	Let's eat pizza. = Shall we eat pizza? = Why don't we eat pizza? = How about pizza? / 　How about eating pizza?	Let's not eat pizza.

That Sounds + Adjective
That sounds great[nice, good, awful, bad].

Unit 10

Past Tense of Be verb (Was/Were)		
Positives	**Negatives**	
I was	I wasn't	
You were	You weren't	
He/She/It was	He/She/It wasn't	
We were	We weren't	
They were	They weren't	
Questions	**Short Answers**	
Was I?	Yes, you were.	No, you weren't.
Were you?	Yes, I was.	No, I wasn't.
Was he/she/it?	Yes, he/she/it was.	No, he/she/it wasn't.
Were we?	Yes, we were.	No, we weren't.
Were they?	Yes they were.	No, they weren't.

Be Busy ~ing
I was busy studying in the library.

Vocabulary Summary

Unit 1

family	parents	husband	wife	daughter
only child	brother	sister	friend	dog
cat	fine	good	great	okay
club	professor	listener	miss	
very well	pretty good	not so[too] good	not so[too] bad	
nothing much	nothing in particular	couldn't be better	couldn't be worse	

Unit 2

California	Hiroshima	London	Liverpool	Manhattan
Miami	Paris	Rome	Seoul	Sydney
Texas	Toronto	address	anytime	call
spell	visit	text	introduce	first name
family[last] name	phone number	e-mail address	write letters	be from ~

Unit 3

badminton	baseball	basketball	boxing	carrot
classical music	tennis	cook	soccer	swim
favorite	guitar	history	movie	meat
iguana	snake			
go camping	go shopping	go to the dentist	move away	play cards
ride a bicycle	wash the dishes	make a public speech		

Unit 4

sunny	fine	rainy(raining)	pouring	storming
snowy(snowing)	chilly	freezing	raincoat	umbrella
rain boots	gloves	scarf	cloudy	windy
mine	yours	his	hers	ours
warm	cool	chilly	blizzard	hot
borrow	cry	laugh	shout	deliver
write a diary	have a good(terrible) time			

Unit 5

morning	noon	afternoon	evening	midnight
today	tomorrow	Sunday	Monday	Tuesday
Wednesday	Thursday	Friday	Saturday	arrive
already	borrow	break	leave	palace
get together	get used to ~	late for ~	move out	

Unit 6

cute	charming	handsome	gorgeous	shy
sad	angry	nervous	embarrassed	scared
cry	panic	relax	tall	short
chubby	thin	slim	slender	straight hair
curly hair	afraid	blush	pony tail	get some rest
take it easy	make oneself at home		cheer up	take one's time
lose weight				

Unit 7

beauty parlor	convenience store	department store	flower shop	gas station
hospital	library	jewelry store	movie theater	park
street	avenue	area	block	
next to	opposite	behind	between	
go[walk] along	go straight ahead	go[walk] up	go[walk] down	
turn right[left]	at the corner	in front of		

Unit 8

cold	fever	sore throat	cough	runny nose
stuffy nose	headache	backache	stomachache	toothache
earache	terrible	awful	matter	wrong sore throat
runny nose	stuffy nose			

Unit 9

attend the meeting		do one's homework		
go mountain climbing		go dancing	go skateboarding	
go to the swimming pool		go to the dentist	go on a diet	take a walk
take pictures	wash clothes	eating habits	rich in protein	
bored	fiber	mineral	onion	terrific
thirsty	eat out			

Unit 10

in the park	at home	at the party	at the airport	in the playground
at school	at the restaurant	at the gym	at the beach	atthe office
in the library	at the hospital	at the church	at the mall	at work
presentation for	on time	clean out the drawer	a part-time job	answer phone calls
busy ~ing	tired - energetic	short - tall	hungry - full	delicious - terrible
hot - cool	anymore	actually	diligent